THE PURE IN HEART

WITNESS LEE

Living Stream Ministry
Anaheim, CA

First Edition, July 2001.

ISBN 0-7363-1339-7

Published by

Living Stream Ministry
2431 W. La Palma Ave., Anaheim, CA 92801 U.S.A.
P. O. Box 2121, Anaheim, CA 92814 U.S.A.

Printed in the United States of America

02 03 04 05 06 07 / 10 9 8 7 6 5 4 3 2

CONTENTS

PREFACE

This book is a collection of messages given by Brother Witness Lee, a servant of the Lord, in Taipei in 1950. It contains ten messages, covering the way for a saved person to progress in life: to be pure in heart, to remove all that covers God's light within him, to confess his sins, to ask for God's enlightenment, to consecrate himself to God, to deal with his conscience, to live before God, and to have a proper service in Christ. These messages have been hidden for half a century; now that they are being published, the abundance of life contained in them is once again released.

CHAPTER ONE

THE PURE IN HEART

Second Corinthians 3:16 says, "But whenever their heart turns to the Lord, the veil is taken away." The veil is related to the heart. One who pursues the Lord and wants to participate in His service must bring his heart with him. Sadly, there is a problem: once a person comes, his heart comes, and his ways of doing things also come with him. We must see that God only wants our heart; all the other things have to be removed and broken by Him. All of our viewpoints and methods have to be broken by God; He just wants our heart. From the very beginning God just has one purpose in His work, that is, to work Himself into us. For this reason, He must gain our heart so that He will be able to work Himself into us.

MAN HAVING THREE PARTS—SPIRIT, SOUL, AND BODY

Man is a vessel created by God for the purpose of containing God. We may use a glass as an illustration. A glass is a vessel created to contain water. For it to be used in any other way is inappropriate. Similarly, in the universe man is a special vessel for containing God. If man does not contain God, there is no meaning to his human existence because man was specially created for God's use. However, how can God put Himself into man? Proverbs 20:27 says, "The spirit of man is the lamp of Jehovah, / Searching all the innermost parts of the inner being." This indicates that we have a spirit within us. First Thessalonians 5:23 says that we human beings are of three parts: spirit, soul, and body. Our outward part is the body, and our inward part is the spirit. In between the spirit and the body is our soul. The soul is our personality, our self, including our mind, will, and emotion. Our feelings of joy, anger, sorrow, and delight are the functions of the soul which belong to the emotion. Our choices and decisions are the functions of the soul, which belong to the will. Our concepts and thoughts are the functions of the soul, which belong to the mind. The soul is the true "I" and what the psychologists refer to as the metaphysical being—something that can be felt but not touched.

Often, certain things may cause the soul of a saved person to be full of pain and sorrow, yet still, deep within his being, there is a joy which is unspeakable. This proves that other than having a soul within our being, there is a spirit deep within us. Hence, sometimes we may be sad because we have a soul, but the reason we can be joyful is that we have a spirit. When our soul feels sorrowful, the Holy Spirit will strengthen us and give us joy from within. Since we have both the soul and spirit, we have two different feelings. This also shows us that we human beings are of three parts: spirit, soul, and body.

THE LINE OF GOD'S LIFE— FROM THE CENTER TO THE CIRCUMFERENCE

The purpose of God's work on us is to work Himself into us. The principle of God's work is to work from the center to the circumference. For example, when we throw a stone into a pond, ripples are stirred up in the water which spread out from the center circle by circle. The working of God in us is also from the center to the circumference. The center of our being is our spirit, and the circumference is our body. The work of God in us is similar to coloring in a circle. He gradually adds color beginning from the center and spreading outward until it is fully colored. He wants to reach our body starting from our spirit.

When we were saved, we used our heart and spirit to receive the Lord Jesus as our Savior, and the Lord's Spirit came into our spirit. As a result, we have God in the center of our being. Before we receive the Lord, we do not have God in us; however, at the very moment we receive Him, the Holy Spirit enters into us, and we have God in us. Originally, we do not have God in our spirit, soul, or body, but when we repent and receive the Lord Jesus as our Savior, God comes in, and we have God's life in us.

Whenever we encounter an outward environment which causes our soul to suffer, we still feel joyful and comforted deep within where the Holy Spirit and the life of God are. This is because the Holy Spirit in our spirit gives us comfort, support, and supply. However, at this point the Holy Spirit is merely in our spirit and has not yet entered into our soul. At the moment of our salvation God began to work in us. Now He wants to spread out from the center of our being, all the way to the circumference, so that the mind, will, and emotion of our soul will possess the element of God. Eventually, He wants to fill our entire being completely. In this way we will not only have God in our spirit, but we will have God in every part of our soul. Our joy, anger, sorrow, and delight will all be filled with God. At that time our viewpoint will be God's viewpoint. Our joy, anger, sorrow, and delight will be God's joy, anger, sorrow, and delight. How is this possible? It is because God is living out from us. We may liken this to a cotton ball absorbing red ink. The red ink saturates the cotton little by little, until finally the whole cotton ball becomes red.

Today no matter how spiritual we are, we are still not wholly spiritual. Only when God's life in us spreads from our spirit to every part of our mind, emotion, will, and even to our body, causing our entire being to be filled with God's life completely and making our body a glorious body, will we be entirely spiritual. But this will be fully accomplished only when the Lord Jesus comes back. At that time our body will be fully transfigured. First Corinthians 15 says that "this corruptible must put on incorruption" (v. 53). Not only will we have God in our spirit and our soul, but we will also have God in our body. This is God's line of life in us.

MAN MUST COOPERATE WITH GOD
AND LET GOD WORK

God wants to work His life into every part of our soul, that is, into our mind, will, and emotion. How does God do this? The basic requirement of the work of God is that man must cooperate with God; man must let God work. It is not that

God does not work, but that many people do not let God work.
When some children are sick, they are not willing to take
any medicine. When their mother takes them to a doctor,
both the doctor and the mother hope that the children will
take the medicine, but they are just unwilling. Similarly, it is
not that God is unwilling to put Himself into us but that we
are reluctant and unwilling.

What then will God do? Doctors and mothers should know
that there are three methods to help a child to take medicine.
First, they can "trick" him. They can cover the medicine with
a sugar coating, and the child will think that he is eating
candy; in fact, though, he is taking in the medicine. Second,
they can make him happy. When the child is happy and satisfied, he will be willing to take in the medicine. All doctors and
nurses use this kind of method to "deceive" their patients, yet
their intention is simply to help the patients and gain their
cooperation. Third, if the child is reluctant to take medicine,
the doctors and nurses can give him a shot. This is a stronger
way. They can do this by restraining his hands and feet, not
allowing him to resist, and then injecting the medicine into
him. For God to fill our inmost part, the methods He uses are
similar to these. Some people may ask, "Does God trick us like
this?" God does not trick us. He is just like the doctors and
nurses, seemingly "deceiving" the patients to take the medicine, but actually trying to gain the cooperation of their
patients. It is the same with God; He wants man to cooperate
with Him.

There was a couple who went to America for school. Both
of them were unbelievers. The wife was the daughter of a
pastor. She had both wealth and position, but she did not
have God, and she felt pain and emptiness within. One day
God gave this couple a very good child. They treasured the
child very much, and they knew that God had given him to
them. The couple said, "If God had not given us this child, we
surely would not have been able to have one by ourselves."
However, they only received the gift but not the God who gave
them the gift. They treasured the child, but they did not trea-
sure God. Two years later the child drowned in a river. The
couple was very sad. They seemed to have lost the heavens

and the earth. It was at this moment that a believer came to them and said, "In the past you only wanted the child that God gave you but not God Himself. You had a child, but he could not give you any comfort." After the couple heard this, they knelt down before God and confessed their sins, saying, "O God, forgive us, for we heard the gospel in the past, but we were not willing to receive You." In this way, they received the Lord and God came into them. God often allows similar things to happen to show us that we need Him.

There was a sister in Shanghai who was a nurse. She was married at the age of forty. She and her husband had a child, and they loved him far more than they loved God. The situation of this sister was like a knotted piece of wood, which is not easily split. Then one day her child died. Many brothers and sisters went to help her. When the child was about to be put into the coffin, his mother was crying and said that she wanted to be put into the coffin with him. When the brothers and sisters saw this situation, they were grieved in their hearts, not knowing what to do. However, a few days later this sister went to see a brother and said, "I truly thank God. The way He has dealt with me is right." After saying this, she burst into tears. If these things had not happened, God would have had no way to enter into her mind, her will, and her emotion. Now, however, God filled her entire being.

TURNING OUR HEART TO GOD
TO BE THE PURE IN HEART

If God wants to work in us but we do not cooperate with Him, He will use some ways to make us willing to cooperate with Him. Here we see that if we want God to work in us, we have to cooperate with Him; otherwise, we are asking for trouble. But what is the way to cooperate with God? First, it is a matter of our heart. If we want to cooperate with God and allow Him to work in us, first of all we must turn our heart to God, for those who are pure in heart shall see God. A pure heart in the Bible refers mainly to a heart that desires God. The object of those who are pure in heart is God Himself. They do not want money, position, or beautiful clothing and expensive perfume. They also do not focus too much on their husband or children. Their heart is solely for God. Matthew says, "Blessed are the pure in heart, for they shall see God" (5:8); and the Psalms say, "Whom do I have in heaven but You? / And besides You there is nothing I desire on earth" (73:25). The pure in heart have a heart so pure that they just want God and nothing other than God.

If Christians are willing to allow God to work in them, the first thing they have to do is to turn their heart to God. God does not have the way to work on many people because their heart is not set on Him. We cannot say that they do not want the Lord. They really do want the Lord, but they also want something other than the Lord Himself. The elderly sisters desire the Lord, but many also desire their children, and many also desire to find a good wife for their son. Many people love the Lord on the one hand, but on the other hand, love money and the respect of the saints. They come to the meeting hall to clean the chairs. This shows that they really love the Lord; however, after they have cleaned the chairs, if the responsible brothers do not show their appreciation of them, they feel uncomfortable. So if we say that they do not love the Lord, we do them an injustice, but if we say that they love the Lord, we do the Lord an injustice. Their inner being is very complicated, but love should be very simple. A wife should love her husband, not for the money that he gives her. In the same way, Christians should love God, not because God gives them money. However, many people love God as the One they can go to when they want to ask for something. Psalm 73:2 says, "But as for me, my feet were nearly turned aside; / My steps had almost slipped." Even the psalmist said that his steps had almost slipped; what is our situation?

Many times we may be perplexed and wonder why those who are pure in heart are often not prosperous, while those who do not love the Lord are often very prosperous. The answer to these questions is made clear when we enter into the sanctuary of God (v. 17). Other people gain only earthly joy and earthly peace, but the pure in heart gain God Himself. This is what a clean heart possesses. We have to bear in mind that the reason why God cannot work in us is that our inner being is not clean enough. It is hard for God to work in us because our heart is not pure. Once our heart is not proper, our focus is also incorrect. This is why the Bible says that whenever our heart turns to the Lord, the veil is taken away (2 Cor. 3:16). For this reason, it is hard to see God's work in many of God's children. All their problems hinge on whether their heart is on money, on their children, or on God. Judging others does not avail, neither does merely searching the Scriptures. Only turning our heart to God is profitable to us. Some people have half of their heart turned to God, while other people have their heart completely turned away from God. We have to bear in mind that how much our heart is for God determines how much work God will do in us. May we all be those who are pure in heart toward Him.

CHAPTER TWO

REMOVING ALL THAT COVERS THE LIGHT

Matthew 5:8 says, "Blessed are the pure in heart, for they shall see God." Second Corinthians 3:16 goes on to say, "But whenever their heart turns to the Lord, the veil is taken away." These two verses reveal that in order for someone to see God and receive His shining, the most important thing is that he must either be one who is already not covered in any way, or he must have his coverings removed. The pure in heart shall see God because they are not covered by anything. When a veil is put on someone's face, it covers his eyes, but when the veil is taken away, he is able to see the light.

REMOVING THE VEIL TO RECEIVE LIGHT

By removing everything that covers him, a person will see light. This is based upon 2 Corinthians 3:16 which reveals that whenever the Corinthians would turn their heart to the Lord, their veil would be taken away. When the heart of the Corinthians was turned away from the Lord, the veil was still on their heart; their turned-away heart was the veil. Whenever the veil was taken away and their heart was turned to the Lord, the Corinthians would receive God's shining. Therefore, the reason man does not receive God's shining is not because God does not shine, but because there is a veil and a covering within man. If man can solve the problem of being covered, then he will see light. Matthew 5:8 says that the pure in heart shall see God, and 1 John 1:5 says, "God is light." Thus, no one can see God without seeing light. God is light, and all those who see light are in God and must be in God alone. However, the requirement of God is that man must be pure in heart. To be pure in heart means that everything that covers the heart has been removed. Once a person's heart is not pure and has mixture, that mixture becomes a covering. Only the pure in heart do not have any covering; only those who do not have any covering can see light.

Psalm 73:1 says, "Surely God is good to Israel, / To those who are pure in heart." This is the psalmist's appreciation. In verse 16 he says, "When I considered this in order to understand it, / It was a troublesome task in my sight." However, when he entered into the sanctuary of God, he understood everything (v. 17). So in verse 25 the psalmist declares, "Whom do I have in heaven but You? / And besides You there is nothing I desire on earth." This is to be pure in heart. One who is pure in heart pursues only the Lord in heaven and desires only the Lord on earth. To be pure in heart is to live on this earth desiring only God and to have no desire other than God. When our heart is single and pure toward God, we are those who are without any covering. Hence, the Bible shows us that in order to see the light, it is necessary to remove the covering.

REMOVING ALL THAT COVERS THE LIGHT

Everything in this universe, besides God Himself, can be a covering to us. First John says that God is light. Thus, anything that is not God Himself can cover the light of God within us. Other than God Himself, there is nothing that is not a covering of the light. Therefore, we all must know that besides God, everything can become a covering to us. Only God Himself is light, and only light itself cannot cover light. We have to remember that all other people, matters, and things outside of God can cover the light. We should not think that good things will not become coverings of the light. In fact, what hinders many people from seeing light is not bad things but many good things.

For example, the pursuit of spirituality is something very high. However, even the pursuit of spirituality can replace God and become a covering of the light, causing one's inner being to be without light. If we are willing to still our heart and to be calm before God, we immediately realize that there is a pile of things covering us, covering the light, and preventing us from seeing what is real. When a person is not pure, it is often the case that although he loves the Lord, his love for the Lord is superficial. He does love the Lord, but at the same time he also loves his face. He does not realize that his love for his face instead of the Lord becomes a covering, hindering him from receiving the light.

There is a saying, "The novices see the outside; the experts see the depths." An experienced fabric seller can tell whether a fabric is a product of America or of Japan merely by touching the fabric with his hands, without even looking at it. A person who serves the Lord is the same; he is an expert at "touching" people. Whenever someone comes to him, without the other person saying anything, he knows his background merely by "touching" him.

The inner sense of a servant of the Lord is the most sensitive part for "touching" others. The most useful tool in serving people is the sense in our spirit. When we contact a brother, we can sense what kind of person he is without having much conversation with him. When we want to speak something to him, within us we first have to weigh, to measure, whether or not he is able to receive our word. If while we "weigh" him, we sense that he will not be able to receive our word, then it is better not to say anything.

Sometimes people come to me and ask me to tell them what their problem is, but because of their dignity I cannot tell them. We should not assume that the ones responsible for the home meetings or small groups are greatly advanced and that they are willing to forsake everything for the Lord. Actually, once we touch their dignity, they may be unable to get through. Once there was a brother who came to me to ask me to identify his problem. I felt that this brother's problem was that he loved his face too much, but I could not tell him this. He urged me again and again, so I tested to see if he could take a word concerning this. I told him, "Your problem is that you never admit your failure." He said, "How do you know?" I said to him that although I had known him for a long time, I had never heard him say, "I am wrong." If a person has been broken and dealt with by God, he should be willing to say, "I am wrong. Please forgive me." But that brother said in response, "I do not think so." He was not willing to lose his face. This is an example of being covered from the light.

In order to help him, I showed him an example, saying, "One day you began to do something with your wife; it was obvious that you were not able to complete it, but you insisted on doing it so that I, your wife, and others would see." He said, "You saw the opposite of the real situation. The situation was not like this." I admitted to him that perhaps I did not see the situation as it really was. Therefore, two months later when this brother came to me again and asked me to identify his problem, I could not say anything to him. Some people are able to put the whole world aside except for their dignity.

The biggest problem among young people is the matter of comparison. If two people are working in the same place and one is praised, the other will feel bothered within. This feeling covers the light. When others receive praise, we have a certain kind of feeling; when we receive praise, we have another kind of feeling. These feelings are a covering—covering the light and causing our heart to not be pure. What is a pure heart? If I have a pure heart, when people say that I am wrong, I have no particular feeling; when people say that I am right, I also have no particular feeling. When people praise me, I have no particular feeling, and when people do not praise me, I also have no particular feeling. I do not desire the praise of others; rather, I desire God Himself. If we want too many things and our desires are too complicated, then anything, even our spiritual pursuit, can become something that covers the light. For instance, some people love to boast, so boasting becomes a great problem to them. Undoubtedly, they are very lovely and learned, but because they do not have light, they just love to boast. Whatever they do, they have to boast a little. This is a covering to them. If we want to see the light, we must remove everything that covers us.

TURNING THE HEART TO THE LORD

Second Corinthians 3:12-18 is a wonderful portion of the New Testament. On the one hand, it says that the sons of Israel are veiled, and on the other hand, it says that whenever their heart turns to the Lord, the veil is taken away. The removal of the veil does not depend on anything other than turning our heart to the Lord. When the veil is not taken away, there is no light, but once the heart turns to the Lord, the veil is taken away. The veil refers to all the things that we pursue other than the Lord. Whenever our heart turns to the Lord, the veil is taken away. All the veils are due to the fact that our heart is not focused on the Lord. Therefore, verse 16 says that whenever our heart turns to the Lord, the veil is taken away. Once our heart turns to the Lord and desires the Lord in a single and pure way, we become a person who is pure in heart. One who is pure in heart does not know anything; he just knows the Lord. He does not desire anything; he just desires the Lord. One who is pure in heart does not covet anything in the world; neither does he covet anything in the spiritual realm. He is able to say, "O Lord, whom do I have in heaven but You? And besides You there is nothing I desire on earth." His heart is so pure and is not covered by any veil. Furthermore, once his veils are taken away, light comes, and immediately he sees. We all must realize what our problem is. Our problem is that our inner being is not pure and that we still have a great deal of mixture in us. Therefore, our heart needs to turn to the Lord.

Some people may ask, How do we know that we are focusing on something other than the Lord? How do we know what these things are? And how do we know if we are focusing on the Lord as well as on something else? Actually, everyone knows already. All the problems hinge on whether or not we are willing to be broken and to receive the dealing of the cross. In the example mentioned before, the brother argued with me and tried to justify himself. I do not believe that he did not have any negative feeling within him while he was arguing. Neither do I believe that a person who loves to boast does not have any similar feeling. They all have this kind of feeling, but the question is whether or not they are willing to receive it.

Second Corinthians 3:16 says, "Whenever their heart turns to the Lord, the veil is taken away." Verse 17 says, "And the Lord is the Spirit; and where the Spirit of the Lord is, there is freedom." When we put these two verses together, they say, "Whenever their heart turns to the Lord...and the Lord is the Spirit." What does this mean? The apostle wrote these two verses so close together because he knew that people might ask him, "You want me to turn to the Lord, but where is the Lord?" The apostle answered this question indirectly by saying that the Lord is the Spirit. When people ask us how it can be possible to know if they have turned their heart to the Lord, we should turn the question back to them and ask them whether or not they have freedom within. Do you think that the arguing brother that I mentioned before has freedom? I believe that the more he argues with me, the less freedom he has within. The more he ignores his inner feeling and refutes my words, the more his spirit within him is bound. Eventually, he will not have any light. Once a person who loves to boast begins to do so, his inner being has no freedom because the Lord Spirit is bound within him. We must ask ourselves, do we prefer to turn to our boasting or to the Lord, who has no freedom within us?

Surely someone who loves money or children more than the Lord has some feeling within him. We all can testify that we do have a particular feeling inside of us when we love money; we feel bound and oppressed within. Then when we open our mouth to pray, others will know that there is something wrong with us—the Lord within us is not free; He is bound in us. If we still love money, or if we love our children more than the Lord, how can we not have an uneasy feeling? However, if we are willing to turn to the Lord, who has been bound within us, we will immediately receive freedom and be full of light. What are our hindrances, and what are the things that we are pursuing other than the Lord? No doubt they are the things that make us feel uneasy. When we feel uneasy or uncomfortable regarding a certain matter, that matter is a hindrance; this is something we are pursuing other than the Lord. We should unreservedly allow the Lord to break it.

When we see the zeal of some young people, we cannot deny that they love the Lord and pursue the Lord. Nevertheless, they still have problems within them. Although everyone is different, some of their problems are quite similar to one another. Last year when they were not willing to pursue the Lord and were not zealous for the Lord, they had a particular problem; this year when they are willing to pursue the Lord and are zealous for the Lord, they still have the same problem. When they are being dealt with in one aspect, they have this fundamental problem; when they are being dealt with in another aspect, the problem is still there. Their problem is that whenever someone else finds fault with what they are doing, they always have an excuse. Even if their mistake is very obvious, they are still not willing to admit it. They should not wait until the Lord comes before they will say, "Sorry, I am wrong." In fact, it is very rare to hear a young person say, "Sorry, I am wrong." When people point out their mistakes, they are not only unwilling to admit them, but they also provide many excuses. This is an example of being covered, for they are reluctant to receive light from within.

If we do not receive light for a long time, we will lose our inner feeling and fall into darkness. When others point out our mistakes, we should be able to say, "Sorry, this is my fault. Please forgive me." If we can do this, we have a clear understanding of light. However, when others find fault with us, we may excuse ourselves, reasoning that our faults are unavoidable. Moreover, when they come to us again, we may continue to defend ourselves. This indicates that our inner being is fully covered and is in darkness. When some people quarrel with their spouse at home, they have an uneasy feeling within them. Actually everyone should have these feelings within, but eventually due to their continual practice of arguing, their inner feeling is lost. Therefore, we should not claim that our actions are reasonable. Even when we do something reasonable, we should not fight for it, because even our "reasonableness" has a little bit of the self in it. As long as we have light and feeling within, we should accept the breaking and the dealing that comes from this light. In this way we will not be in darkness.

We need to repent to the Lord for our inability to see the light. In our church life we read the Bible every day, yet we may not have light. We have the Bible in our mind, yet there is no light within us. We also serve the Lord fervently, but there is no light or reality in our serving, and we do not know why we are serving. Not only so, while we work, our inner being is full of confusion and without light. We live the so-called spiritual life day by day without any fresh spiritual vision and our inner being seems to lack something. Every day we rise up early to read the Bible. Every day we visit people and take care of them, yet we may not have any fresh seeing or fresh feeling within.

A person who lives before the Lord, however, should be shining and fresh every day. Whenever he comes to the Lord, he receives light. This is not the light that he saw yesterday but new light that he sees today. His inner being is always clear and certain about the direction of his serving and the move of the Holy Spirit. Not only does he know the direction of the move of the church, but he also knows God's purpose for the church on the earth. His inner feeling is always fresh and bright. This kind of person is always learning something new and receiving new shining each day. When people contact him, although outwardly he may not seem to be very affectionate, his inner being is soft and fresh, as clear as crystal, and transparent. Some who are saved, even having received grace from the Lord, would behave in a rough way; their problem is that their heart is not pure enough for the Lord. They are too complicated within, and so when a feeling comes, they are not willing to receive it. We all have the feeling within us, yet often we are not willing to receive the breaking that comes with the feeling. This unwillingness is the rejection of light.

"WHERE THE SPIRIT OF THE LORD IS, THERE IS FREEDOM"

Man does not enter into darkness abruptly; rather, he does so gradually. The setting of the sun is always from morning to afternoon, from afternoon to dusk, and from dusk to evening. Evening, however, is still not the darkest time. All men who enter into darkness do so in a gradual way, without any feeling that it is happening. It is in such an unconscious way that man gradually drifts toward something other than the Lord. This is the result of a lack of light within. Hence, if we feel uneasy or confused in a certain area, this is where we need to receive light and breaking from the Lord. If we receive continuous breaking before the Lord in this way, the light within us will shine brighter and brighter, because the veils in us will be gradually taken away.

For example, suppose I am a person who loves to justify myself. When you come to tell me something and I want to explain the situation to you, my inner being will feel uncomfortable. At that moment, I should immediately receive this feeling, bow my head, and tell the Lord, "O Lord, I will not say anything; even if they misunderstand me, I will still not say anything." We should not disobey the inner feeling and shining, neither should we disobey the inner vision. Once we have a feeling from the Lord, we should submit to it. Many of us can testify that whenever we stop, right away there is freedom in our spirit. Where the Spirit of the Lord is, there is freedom. Some people are always asking, How do we know if our heart is turned to the Lord? We know that our heart is turned to the Lord when our spirit is free. When we are quarreling with our husband or our wife and we sense that our inner being is not free, we should bow our head immediately and tell the Lord, "O Lord, I would not quarrel anymore." Once you stop, your inner being will be free, your spirit will be released, and you will be able to praise. If we are like this every morning, then our daily living will be fresh. On the contrary, if we continue to quarrel and to disobey the feeling, I am afraid that throughout the whole day, from the morning to the evening, our inner being will be in confusion and darkness, and our spirit will not be free. Whenever our heart turns to the Lord, the veil is taken away.

CHAPTER THREE

THE FIRST STEP AFTER SALVATION— PURGING OUT THE LEAVEN

SALVATION AS THE BEGINNING

Once a person is saved and becomes a Christian, he should know what steps he needs to take to progress in the Christian life. The Bible tells us that after a Christian is saved, he has Christ's life in him. Receiving the Lord's life, however, is only the beginning, not the end. To be saved and baptized and to possess Christ's life is the first step of salvation. Although a newly saved believer has the Lord's life in him, this life in him is very shallow; he does not yet have much progress in the Lord's life. Many people have been saved for years. After so much time they should have deep and far-reaching progress in their Christian life, yet because they have not received the adequate leading and have not had the proper pursuit, they do not have much growth in life. They are continually treading over the same ground and walking in circles. This can be likened to someone who walks in the city of Taipei from morning to evening every day for five years, but never leaves the city limits, because the whole time he just walks in circles. He walks much, but he never advances; he spends much energy, but he never makes any progress. Why is this? It is because he does not take a straight path but walks in circles the whole time. In contrast to this, it takes only a few hours to travel by train from Taipei to Kaohsiung because the way goes straight and forward the whole time.

Many Christians, however, are not like this. Although they listen to messages, read the Bible, and attend meetings all the time, they still have not made any progress. They were like this five years ago, and today they are still the same.

They seem to have a little understanding of doctrine, but concerning the Lord's life, they are still ignorant. Even though they may understand Genesis 1, Matthew 1, and many teachings in the Bible, they do not understand the way of the Lord. Although they study the Bible and have a share in Christ, they are strangers to the Lord's way. They are totally ignorant of what it means to follow the Lord and take His way.

Progressing in the Christian life is similar to taking a train from Taipei down to Kaohsiung in the south. After the first station—Panchiao, and the second station—Taoyuan, we eventually will arrive in Kaohsiung. All those who are advanced in the Lord's way know that the Lord's way is just like this. The way of the Lord is "station by station," with different levels and different steps.

ALLOWING GOD TO DO THE WORK OF CLEANSING

The first thing a saved one who wants to take the Lord's way must pay attention to is keeping himself absolutely clean and free from all defilement. We may use an illustration. When a cup is dropped into a trashcan, after it is picked out, can we use it right away? Of course, we cannot. If we want to use it, we first have to wash and sanitize it thoroughly, and then we can use it. Before we have washed it thoroughly, we certainly cannot use it. If the cup is not washed, then it has no function and cannot be used for anything. In the same way, we are like the cup; if we are not willing to allow the Lord to cleanse us, the Lord cannot do anything with us. If we want the Lord to work in us, we first need to be cleansed by Him thoroughly.

We thank the Lord for saving so many of us. Before we were saved, we all had fallen into the trashcan of the world. Actually, to compare the world to a trashcan is to overestimate its worth. We should say that the world is like a manure pit. In fact, it is even smellier than a manure pit. Hence, before we were saved, our entire being was defiled and full of "germs." None of us was clean in our thoughts or emotions; we were altogether filthy and evil within and without. However, one day the Lord came; His gospel reached us, His voice entered into our heart, His Spirit sympathized with us, and we were saved. The Lord rescued us and separated us from sin and evil. Although we have been saved, all our defilement and "germs" have not been totally removed. They still are present in our flesh and conduct. Therefore, the first step that we must take after being saved is to allow God to cleanse us. If we do not allow God to cleanse us, we will have no way to start walking on the way of the Lord. Moreover, if we do not allow the Lord to wash us, the Lord will have no way to work in us.

Whether we are newly saved or we have been saved for years, we have to take such a word. Although many of us were "picked out of the trash" by the Lord many years ago, until this day we have not allowed the Lord to do a cleansing work on all the "germs" and defilement within us. Although we may understand more doctrines, be familiar with more Christian regulations, and know more Christians than we did in the past, we have not walked a step further. The problem is here: although we allowed the Lord to "pick us out of the trash," we have never allowed Him to make us clean and fresh. All the defilement and "germs" are still within us. So in order for the Lord to work in us, He has to wait for our consent. When we give the Lord our consent, He will do the cleansing work in us. If we are unwilling or reluctant, then the Lord will have no way to lead us or do the cleansing work in us.

KEEPING THE FEAST OF THE PASSOVER
AND THE FEAST OF UNLEAVENED BREAD

The children of Israel in the Old Testament typify us, who are saved by grace. Their keeping of the Feast of the Passover typifies our being saved by grace. They were saved by killing a lamb and putting the blood on the lintel and the doorposts. Today when we receive the Lord and "put His blood on us," the judgment of God and the wrath of God pass over us, and we are saved. Immediately following the Feast of the Passover, the children of Israel kept another feast, which is called the Feast of Unleavened Bread. There was no gap in time between these two feasts. The Feast of Unleavened Bread was right

after the Feast of the Passover. The children of Israel kept
the Feast of the Passover in the evening on the fourteenth
day of the first month of the year. On this night they started
to keep the Feast of the Passover, and on the very next night
they immediately began to keep the Feast of Unleavened Bread.
The beginning of the Feast of the Passover could also be said
to be the beginning of the Feast of Unleavened Bread. Hence,
once we are saved and we keep the Feast of the Passover, we
also should keep the Feast of Unleavened Bread immediately.
First Corinthians 5 says, "Purge out the old leaven that you
may be a new lump, even as you are unleavened" (v. 7a). This
means that once we are saved, we should purge out the old
leaven. What is it to purge out the leaven? In the Bible leaven
refers to corruption. The reason meal rises is because of the
leaven within it. There is an element of corruption in leaven
which enables it to leaven the whole meal in several hours. So
the leaven in the meal refers to corruption.

All fallen human beings live a corrupted life. Some people
may ask, What do you mean by a corrupted life? What is
the leaven in our living? We may use a young person as an
illustration. We all know the situation of the young people. A
teenager's mind may be very clean and pure, but once he goes to
high school, he may begin to read romance novels. Then these
romance novels begin to enter into him as leaven, until one
day this leaven in him becomes sour and smelly, causing this
person, who was originally so pure, to be gradually corrupted
within.

Some people say that movies are good and that they can be
very helpful if they are used for educational purposes. It is
true that in some aspects movies may be quite useful, but
unfortunately, in these days people misuse movies. All parents
know that today the market is filled with movies that do not
enlighten the minds of the young people; rather, they stimu-
late the evil in them. Many times although the movie itself is
good, due to the improper environment in which it is viewed,
many problems arise. We have to know that theaters are dirtier
than pigsties. Some young people have asked me indignantly,
"Is it also wrong to watch films about science or history?"
There is nothing wrong with watching films about science or

history if they are shown at school, but we should not go to theaters, because that kind of place is too dirty.

We may also illustrate this point using a calendar. A calendar is something good and indispensable, but some people like to print improper pictures on calendars. What is this? This is leaven, which is subtly imparted into man, and which causes many young people to turn sour and smelly. Doctors and biologists both tell us that the whole world is full of germs, that is, full of leaven. This is a world of corruption. The thoughts and deeds of so many people have a corrupting influence. Just by existing in this corrupted world, regardless of whether we are conscious of it or not, we are continually being contaminated by defiling things and germs. When we were saved, the wrath of God passed over us. Nevertheless, we are still full of germs and corruption. How can the Lord work in people like us? He cannot. If we want the Lord to work in us, first we must allow the Lord to cleanse us.

After the children of Israel kept the Feast of the Passover, they kept the Feast of Unleavened Bread right away. Today many Christians keep the Feast of the Passover, but there are very few who also keep the Feast of Unleavened Bread. One time I was invited to a love feast. As I entered into the house, I saw something there which made me very uncomfortable. If you always live in an environment of fresh air, once you enter into a house which has a scarcity of fresh air, you will immediately feel very uncomfortable. Your feeling will be very sensitive. However, for those who are used to living in that kind of environment, not only will they be unaware of the lack of fresh air, but they will even say that you are strange. I was a guest that day, so I did not feel that it was appropriate to say anything. We all sat there singing and praising God, but there was a calendar with an improper picture on it hanging on the wall. This was like eating a great meal beside a dunghill; the taste was disgusting.

Today many people are truly saved, but they have not purged out the leaven within them. If a small and lowly slave of God like me felt uncomfortable when I entered into that house, how could God Himself be comfortable there? A number of other Christians were also there, yet none of them had any feeling. While the people in this house read the Bible, there was something unclean hanging on their wall. This shows that this family has never purged out the leaven or seriously walked the Lord's way. God has no way to do a deeper work in this kind of people.

EXAMPLES OF PURGING OUT THE LEAVEN

We who are saved should all be serious about taking this way. Before the young people are saved, they love to read romance novels, but after they are saved, all these things should either be thrown away or burned. They should never give these books to their classmates. If they give them to their classmates, they are not doing their classmates a favor; rather, they are doing them harm. In 1944, I went to Weihaiwe to preach the gospel. The majority of the congregation there worked as customs officials. Nearly all of their wives were saved, yet their houses were filled with either mah-jongg games or Chinese dominoes. After they were saved, they did not have any peace within, so they came and asked me, "We have mah-jongg tiles of very good quality, and they all cost a lot of money. What should we do with them?" I asked in return, "Why do you come to ask me?" They replied, "It is because we do not feel peaceful." Then I told them, "If you have no peace, then why do you still need to ask me? If you have already smelled something stinking, do you still ask people whether or not you should eat it? If you have already smelled the stinking odor of mah-jongg, you do not need to ask people whether or not you should play it." They answered, "Then we had better give them to other people." To give your mah-jongg tiles away is even worse than being a bandit. A bandit who robs people's money only does harm to them for a short while, but to give your mah-jongg tiles away may ruin someone's life and harm people for two or three generations. So finally, they went back, spread this word amongst one another, and gathered together all their mah-jongg games. Then I said, "You all should burn your mah-jongg tiles as a testimony for the Lord." Then they put their mah-jongg tiles together, piled them up, and while we were giving messages inside the house, they burned all the mah-jongg tiles, Chinese dominoes, and dice in the backyard. This is an example of purging out the leaven.

In 1938, I was staying with someone in Peiping (Beijing) who worked in the Union Hospital. One day he told me that he wondered if the Lord was happy with his silk umbrella that he had in his living room. I was younger than he was, so I respectfully asked him, "After you have spent so much money to get it, why do you now think that it is not good?" He answered, "The umbrella itself is not the problem. The problem is that the umbrella has dragons on it. Do you think that something with dragons on it should be kept in a Christian's home?" Then I told him that since the first day I entered into his house, whenever I saw those four dragons, I felt very uncomfortable within. This brother's feeling came as a result of reading the book of Revelation. When he read that the devil is a dragon, he asked himself, "If I belong to God, why do I still allow something of Satan to remain in my home?" Satan is very deceptive. This is the reason why people today not only have pictures of dragons, but they also wear dragon ornaments, perform the dragon dance, and even wear clothing with dragons embroidered on it. They are totally occupied with dragons.

In 1936, when I was in Tientsin, a sister invited some of us for dinner. This sister's husband was a very famous architect, and the ceiling of her dining room was filled with dragon paintings. Her husband was not at home that day, and we went to her home for dinner. She said that whenever she ate in that dining room, she felt very uncomfortable. I asked her why, and she told me that it was because of the dragons on the ceiling. Then I asked her why she did not like dragons when everyone else likes dragons. Everyone has the image of a dragon either on their teapots or on their clothes. She told me that because she was a child of God, she should not allow such things to remain in her home, but that since her husband was not willing to remove them, it was out of her control. I consoled her by saying that if it is not up to us, then it is not our business.

Since we are saved, we should allow the Lord to enlighten us so that we may see if there is anyone that we have wronged or treated unrighteously. If we have done so, we have to deal with any problems we have with them thoroughly. In addition, if we have obtained something in an unrighteous way, whether it is from someone in our own household or from work, we have to deal with this matter absolutely. If we are willing to go to the Lord and check with ourselves completely, we will find that our entire being is full of leaven. One time, Dr. F. B. Meyer, an American, went to England to preach. He said that there was no way for a Christian to be blessed if he merely listened to sermons day after day yet was unwilling to be dealt with and had no feeling when he stole money from his manager or spent his company's funds. After that sermon all the bank drafts of the surrounding post offices were sold out in a few hours. Why did this happen? This happened because so many people, after seeing their unrighteousness, went to buy bank drafts so that they could pay back the money that they had taken. In that meeting Dr. Meyer used a young man as an example. He said, "This young man has stolen three pounds and eighteen shillings from his master and even until now he has not returned the money. Then he asked the young man, "Do you have peace within?" Later someone invited Dr. Meyer for a meal. The young man was waiting for him there and told him, "Some years ago I really stole three pounds and eighteen shillings from my master, and I have no peace within. I have purchased a check for three pounds and eighteen shillings and have enclosed it in an envelope to return it to my master. Please tell me, am I doing the right thing?"

One time Charles Spurgeon used an illustration in his preaching, saying, "There is a young man here who is wearing a pair of gloves that he stole, and he should return them." When he spoke such a word, he said it without any particular intention, but after he spoke, a young man came up to him and said, "The gloves that I am wearing really were stolen from my master. How did you know?" Spurgeon said, "I did not know anything. When I was speaking, I just was inspired to say that." Many Christians have no problem with their salvation, but they have never dealt with all their unrighteous possessions. If we want to follow the Lord in a serious way, we should deal with all the idols, the ancestral tablets, and the stolen things in our homes.

Many years ago in Kaifeng, Honan Province, there was a sister who had an image of Jesus in her home. She bowed down to worship the image every day and at every meal took some food to offer to the image. Later, she was possessed by demons. A sister who knew her wrote to me and asked, "Can we worship an image of Jesus? Why is this sister possessed by demons even though she worshipped an image of Jesus?" I replied to her that we should not worship even an image of Jesus. We have to use our spirit to worship Jesus Himself. The Gospel of John shows us that when we worship the Lord in spirit and in truthfulness, He will accept us. We should not worship any image, even the image of Jesus, because there are demons behind all these kind of images, even behind the image of Jesus.

BEING CLEAN MATERIAL IN THE LORD'S HAND

We need to pray much and to come back to God. We need to let Him enlighten us and show us if there is anything in our homes, in our being, or in our surroundings that is unpleasing to Him. For example, before some people were saved, their mothers-in-law were a great suffering to them, and they did not like them. Once they are saved, however, this dislike has to be removed. The dislike of the mothers-in-law toward their daughters-in-law also has to be removed. In short, if we dislike anyone or are holding a grudge against anyone—whether they are family, friends, or colleagues—we should confess and thoroughly deal with any problems that are between us. In this way, even if we do not preach the gospel to them, they will be saved through our behavior.

After one sister believed in the Lord, she felt very unpeaceful when she recalled all the times that she had been hard on her daughter-in-law. She desired that her daughter-in-law would be saved, but she was not bold enough to preach the gospel to her. She came to see me, and I said to her, "You persecuted your daughter-in-law before you were saved, do you think she will listen to you now? You should confess to her." She replied, "I am her mother-in-law, how can I confess to my daughter-in-law?" I asked her whether she wanted the Lord or to preserve her face, whether she wanted her daughter-in-law to be saved or she wanted her to go to hell? She said, "In the past I persecuted her; if I confess to her, and later she persecutes me, what will I do?" I told her that she had to trust in the Lord to grant her the grace in this matter. A few days later she came back to me and said, "After I confessed to my daughter-in-law, she cried, and I also cried. Then the two of us knelt down to pray together, and she was saved." Do you see this? Sometimes we can get people saved even without preaching the gospel. We may be sloppy, but our God is never sloppy. We should not be careless or excuse ourselves in these matters; rather, we should carefully purge out all the leaven. In this way one day our whole being will be absolutely clean and free from all defilement within and without. In addition, everything in our family will also be clean. A person who is free from all defilement is clean material in the Lord's hand.

CHAPTER FOUR

CONFESSING OUR SINS
AND ASKING FOR ENLIGHTENMENT

DEALING WITH BOTH
OUTWARD SINS AND INWARD SINS

After a person is saved, if he wants to make progress in life, he must carefully purge out all leaven. This means that he must deal with every situation that is improper in the eyes of the Lord and every matter that is condemned by the Lord. However, he should not only deal with the outward things, but he should confess to the Lord, from deep within, all his inward sins.

Man always has more inward problems than outward problems. He may have many outward problems that are condemnable, but his inward problems and his inward evil far exceed his outward problems. His outward problems are related merely to behavior, but his inward problems are related to his mind, opinion, and even more, to his self. It is possible for a person to be wrong inwardly but not to be wrong outwardly. This means that a person may be full of sins within, and yet outwardly he does not behave in a sinful way. Inside of man there are sin, iniquity, and darkness, but outwardly these things may not seem to be expressed at all. Therefore, if a person wants to grow in life after he has been saved, he should deal with outward sins and improper matters, but he should continually come to the Lord to deal with his real inner condition. When God deals with us and cleanses us, His focus is on our inward being.

A person may outwardly appear to be right but inwardly be altogether wrong and unrighteous. In the Gospels the Lord rebuked the Pharisees, saying, "You resemble whitewashed

graves, which outwardly appear beautiful but inwardly are
full of dead men's bones and all uncleanness" (Matt. 23:27).
This means that some people are like whitewashed graves:
They appear to be beautiful on the outside, but they do not
want others to know their real inward condition, and they
would not allow others to see the filthiness of their inner
being. Much of man's outward behavior is condemnable, but
his inward evil is many times more deserving of condemna-
tion. Man's inner need is far greater than his outward need.
Many times after a person is saved, outwardly speaking, he is
very good and is almost blameless, but two or three years
later, he still does not have much progress in life. This is
because his problem is not something outward but inward.
His outward behavior is correct, yet his inner being is wrong.
Most of our outward behavior is done before men, yet our
inner being is before God. Man should confess not only his
outward sins before God, but even more, he should confess
his inward sins. When God shines on us, He shines not only
on our outward behavior, but also on our inner being.

BEING ENLIGHTENED BY GOD TO CONFESS OUR SINS

Some have been saved for a long time, yet they have never
had a time of confession before God. We all confess that the
Lord Jesus is our Savior, but until today we still may not have
confessed all our inward sins before God. Some may say that
they do not sense that they are sinful. Of course, this word is
not false; a person can be full of sins but still not have
any sense that he is sinful. According to the fact, he is full of
sins; but according to his feeling, he does not sense that he is
sinful. Before God he is full of sins, but in his own feeling he
does not have any sense that he is sinful.

One day in Shanghai, when I entered into the church
business office, everyone laughed at me when they saw me. I
asked them what the matter was. Then a brother brought me
to a mirror, and I saw that I had made myself dirty without
knowing when I did it and without having any feeling about
it. In reality, I had made myself dirty, yet in my feeling, I was
still clean. Many people are like this before God. They are, in
fact, full of uncleanness, yet they still feel that they are good.

Their subjective feeling is far from the fact. There are many examples of this in the Bible. Before a person meets God, he thinks that he is good, but once he touches God, immediately he realizes that he is wrong. Why is this? This is because God is light, and God is like a mirror. Everyone who sees light finds himself sinful before God. The reason a person can see anything, including his own face, is also related to light. For example, if a house is dark and there is no light, even though it may be full of rubbish, no one will sense that it is dirty. However, once a beam of light shines into the house, we will be able to see clearly. If the light is strong enough, we will be able to see even the dust clearly. Bacteria can be seen clearly under a microscope; they cannot escape being seen. Many doctors say that under strong enough light and a powerful microscope, everything a person sees will look dirty.

Every person is sinful before God, but not everyone can see that he is sinful. In the Old Testament once a person came to God, he immediately sensed that he was sinful. When Isaiah the prophet was enlightened, he immediately found that he was unclean. When seraphim from heaven were saying, "Holy, holy, holy," Isaiah said, "Woe is me, for I am finished! / For I am a man of unclean lips, / And in the midst of a people of unclean lips I dwell" (Isa. 6:3, 5). There are at least four things in us which are unclean: our upper lip, our lower lip, our tongue, and our throat. Some people may say, "This is not true; my lips, my tongue, and my throat are all very clean." However, one day when we are truly enlightened by God, we will see that there is no other part of our body that sins more than our lips.

No matter who a person is, once God comes to him, he will confess his sins. Even two hours will not be enough time for him to confess all his sins. Even though we do not know how many sins our tongue and our lips have committed, we do know that we have said things that we should not have said, and that our speaking is often mixed with a bit of evilness and wickedness. As long as a person's lips are clean, he is a clean person. Even today, whose lips have not sinned from morning to this moment? Some may say that they are right and that they do not have sins. Yet when someone really touches God, he will immediately see that he does not have only a few individual sins but piles upon piles of sins. After he has confessed some of his sins, he will still have more to confess. In fact, there will always be more to confess.

One of my gospel friends told me that before he was saved, he thought that he was a perfect gentleman. I also admit that his temperament was one of a righteous gentleman. However, one day he became sick and began to suffer from several diseases: high blood pressure, heart disease, lung disease, and so forth. After he had stayed in the hospital for a long time, he still had not recovered. One day he became really desperate and started to consider, while lying on his bed, what kind of person he was. The more he thought about himself, the more he found himself good; the more he assessed himself further, the more he still found himself good. At that moment, however, he saw a Bible beside him. At that time he had not yet believed in Jesus, and he did not know the meaning of salvation. He opened the Bible, read a little, and suddenly, he discovered that something was wrong in his being—something that he had never found before. He realized that there was a thought in him that was not right, so he confessed this sin before God. Right after he confessed this sin, a second feeling came, causing him to confess a second sin. Then a third feeling also came and he confessed a third, then a fourth, and then a fifth sin. He was confessing his sins in this way, until eventually he lost track of how many sins he had confessed. After a while he felt that because he had so many sins, he should not continue to confess while lying on the bed, so he rose up and prostrated himself in front of his bed. After he had confessed more sins, he took his hands off the bed and entirely prostrated himself on the floor, weeping and confessing at the same time. For at least three hours, he felt that the more he confessed his sins, the more sins he had to confess. In the past he had not sensed that he was wrong, but on that day his sense was completely different. In the beginning he only felt that he was a little bit wrong. But once he made one confession, another sin came; once he made another confession, the third one came. This continued until he forgot about time—confessing on the one hand and weeping on the other. Although he was quite a strong man and was accomplished in his career, he was saved! His salvation was not a casual one, but one in which he confessed all his sins.

Luke 5 records Peter's story. Originally, Peter did not realize that he was sinful, but when the Lord shined on him, he immediately said, "Depart from me, for I am a sinful man, Lord" (v. 8). In the Old Testament Job was one who also did not realize his sins until God shined on him. His three friends told him that he must have sinned before God, but Job did not agree and wanted to argue with God to see where his sins were (Job 5—6). This shows that Job was in darkness; he had never touched God or seen the light. However, at the end of the book of Job, he met God and said to Him, "I had heard of You by the hearing of the ear, / But now my eye has seen You; / Therefore I abhor myself, and I repent / In dust and ashes" (42:5-6). Why did he repent? He repented because he saw his uncleanness. All of us are filthy and unclean before God. A person who has touched God sees his filthiness, and one who is enlightened by God senses his uncleanness. But one who has never touched God or seen the light, even though he is filthy and unclean, does not have any feeling of filthiness. Every time a person touches God, he will see that he is full of sins and that he is a constitution of sin.

Over fifteen hundred years ago there was a man named Augustine. When he was young, he lived a life of debauchery. His mother loved the Lord devoutly and always prayed for her son. One day Augustine suddenly had a feeling and asked himself why he was living in debauchery and not turning to God. At that moment he repented. To his surprise, that day he discovered that the more he confessed his sins, the more sins he had. It seemed that before he began to confess, there was not much sin, but the more he confessed, the more severe and abundant the sins became. Later, he wrote a book called *Confessions,* in which he describes his experience of confession. He confessed his sins to the extent that he said something like, "Even the regret in my confession needs to be forgiven by God; even the tears that I shed for the sorrow of my sins need to be washed with the precious blood." Can you imagine the extent to which this person confessed? Even though he had already confessed everything, he still felt that even the regret in his confession needed to be forgiven by the Lord.

A person who is before God and who touches God should see that he is sinful. The more he confesses his sins, the more he senses his filthiness; the more he senses his filthiness, the more he comes to God; and the more he comes to God, the more he finds himself sinful. Every saved one, from the moment God leads him to walk this way, has to pass through this experience. From the time we were saved until today, have we ever had a thorough confession before God? This is a very serious question. Many people do not have any problem with their salvation, but it is questionable whether or not they have ever had a thorough confession.

The first time I thoroughly confessed my sins after my salvation was not just for an hour or two, but for a very long period of time. I was enlightened by God to such an extent that even sitting made me feel guilty. It seemed that if I said yes, I sinned, and if I said no, I also sinned. We all were born unclean. Every one of our thoughts and intentions is unclean. When a baby is born and first starts to make noises, his mouth is very pure. But gradually as he learns to speak, his mouth is no longer pure. After he begins to go to elementary school, when you ask him something, he will roll his eyes. Then when he speaks you know that his speaking is with a motive. Any word which is uttered with a motive is unclean.

From 1931 to the present, I have confessed my sins almost every day. One time I was really bothered by a certain matter and I went to confess before God. At the end of my time of confession two sentences came to me that I had never heard before. In response I prayed, "O God, before You I am not merely dirty, I am basically a pile of filth. It is not only that I was a clean person who was defiled and became unclean; not only so, Lord, I am a being constituted with uncleanness. O God, I am not just false, but my whole being is constituted with falsehood." I was enlightened by God to the extent that I realized that I am a constitution of uncleanness, and I am a constitution of falsehood. It was these two sentences which enlightened me. We are not only sinful but we are a constitution of sin.

When God enlightens us, we immediately see our filthiness and evilness. If we have never allowed God to enlighten us, we have not walked, or progressed, even one step before God. When God wants us to walk a step further, He must first enlighten us and cleanse us. Anyone who has never been enlightened thoroughly, no matter how long he has been saved, how much doctrine he understands, or how deeply he knows the Bible, although he is saved, he has never walked one step on the path of God. God's first step in enlightening us is always to cleanse us thoroughly.

CONDITIONS IN WHICH ONE IS ENLIGHTENED

People may be in a variety of conditions when they are enlightened by God. Some people do not have a heart for the Lord after they are saved. As a result, when they are happy, they come to the meetings; and when they are happy, they pray; but when they are depressed, they neither meet nor pray. Often, however, when these kind of people are walking on the street or studying, they suddenly have a feeling within them that they should go to God to pray. Once they pray, they immediately sense that they are sinful, and the more they confess, the more they find themselves full of sins. In this way they are revived by the Lord, and many people may wonder what has happened to them. Once they are enlightened within and stirred up by the Lord, they walk their first step right away—they repent, confess their sins, cleanse themselves, and start to read the Bible. The more they read the Bible, the more they are filled with light. As a result, they love to preach the gospel. In the beginning they did not have a heart for God, but they were chosen and enlightened by God.

There is another kind of person, whose inner condition is exposed when he is listening to a message. At that time he makes a thorough confession and is full of freshness. Someone else may be drawn by hearing the testimonies of other people. As a result, he goes to God to ask for His shining. Eventually, he also is enlightened by God and makes a thorough confession. Another kind of person, after fellowshipping with the saints, feels that he should go to God and be enlightened by Him. As a result, he also receives the shining and thus thoroughly confesses his sins. There is still another kind of person, who receives the feeling that he is sinful when he is in a prayer meeting where either a small or large number of people are praying. When he receives this feeling he thoroughly confesses and also receives the shining. Another kind of person may hear the exhortation of other people and realize that for a Christian to progress in life he must thoroughly confess his sins. As a result, he prays, "O God, I pray that You would shine on me and forgive all my sins." He prays in this way for one or two days, and on the third day, God truly shines on him. Finally, there is a certain kind of person who prays and God gradually shows him that he is sinful.

A resolution is an expression of our seeking before God. Thus, we should all come back to God and tell Him, "O God, I need Your shining. So I ask You to shine on me and show me my sins. I know that there is a principle here: If I am not enlightened and my sins are not exposed, there is no way for me to grow in life." This kind of prayer is one that God is very willing to answer and one that He will answer quickly.

One other kind of person may become enlightened when he asks God for something. God does not give it to him, but instead shows him that he is wrong. This kind of situation is common with children. A child may go to his father for a piece of candy and stretch out his small hands and say in a spoiled way, "Daddy, give me a piece of candy." Then the father would say, "Look at your hands, they are so dirty. Go wash them." Then the child may wash his hands and again ask for a piece of candy. The father then may take out a mirror and ask him to look at his dirty face, and the child would go to wash his face. After he washes his face, he may ask for a piece of candy again. Then the father will show him his dirty neck and dirty clothes. So eventually, after he washes his neck and changes his clothes, his whole being is clean. It is the same with many people when they go to pray before God; they ask God for this and that. God not only does not answer them, but He also shows them how unclean they are. Not until then do they know what it is to follow God, to forsake the world, and to reject sin. And it is only at that time that they will have a start in their spiritual life.

If a person does not have this experience of being enlightened, then he will at most understand some mere doctrines and will have never started on his spiritual path. He will not have any hatred toward sin; neither will he have any feeling toward filthiness. He will stay this way until the day when God shines on him and shows him his sinful condition, and he begins to confess his sins. This kind of feeling toward his sinful condition always lasts for a few years rather than for a few days. In addition, this feeling toward his corruptness, evil, and wrongdoing will keep him coming to God for His shining and cleansing.

SPECIFIC CONFESSIONS

After the period that included the years 1931 to 1935, whenever I went to God to ask for something, this prayer always lasted for only two minutes. For example, when I would pray, "O God, please solve this problem for me," it would take only half a minute to pray such a prayer. Prior to this half a minute, however, it would take me twenty to thirty minutes to confess my sins. When I saw how sinful I was, before I could ask the Lord to solve my problem, I had to confess my sins. After twenty or thirty minutes of confession, I had thoroughly confessed all the sins within me. As a result, I had peace in my conscience, and there was no barrier between my spirit and God. By that time I could be almost face to face with God, telling God boldly and easily, "O God, I am cleansed by the precious blood of Your Son. O God, I have a problem, I ask You to solve this problem for me." Then, God would immediately answer this kind of prayer.

When we pray we are often unclear, and do not know God's will. The key to knowing God's will, however, is to make a thorough confession of our sins. After doing this we will be clear. Anyone who is insensitive to God is also insensitive to sin. We should try praying a simple prayer: When we are walking on the street or at home, we should tell God, "O God, may You shine on me and expose all my sins." Then one day, the light will reach you, and you will sense that you are wrong. No one will tell you that you are wrong outwardly, but inwardly you will sense that you are wrong. Then you will go to God to confess your mistakes. If you realize that you have offended your parents, you will go to God and say, "O God, in the past, I offended my parents in a certain matter, please forgive me." We have to confess our mistakes specifically.

If a wife has committed many mistakes and offended her husband, she has to confess them specifically before God, telling Him the specific matters in which she has wronged her husband or her children. It is the same with a husband. He has to thoroughly confess the specific matters in which he has wronged his wife or his company. In addition, all of our inner intentions and inner thoughts have to be confessed one by one. There is a Western sister who always exhorts people to confess their sins. One day she heard someone pray, "O God, I have so many sins, please forgive me." Then this sister said, "Do not throw such a big bundle to the Lord Jesus. You have to open it up and count the contents item by item." This bundle includes everything; you cannot just say one sentence, "O Lord, I am a great sinner." You need to count the contents item by item, saying, "O Lord, I have wronged my brother in a certain matter. O Lord, I have wronged my husband on a certain occasion, and I have wronged my children at a certain time." In this way, we will see that our sins are exceedingly many, and we will be under the light. Today people are living in darkness and do not have any sense of sin; even though they confess their sins every day, they still do not have any sense of sin.

THE PATH OF LIFE BEGINNING WITH CONFESSION

Here is the problem of many people: Owing to a lack of light, they do not have any feeling. Many people arrive at work at nine or nine-thirty in the morning, even though their company clearly stipulates that they should arrive at eight o'clock, yet when they fill out their attendance cards, they indicate that they were on time. Once a saint asked me, "What should I do in this situation?" I told him, "If your company requires you to work at eight o'clock, you should arrive at eight; if you arrive at nine o'clock, you should write that down." This is to be a true Christian. Today the pitiful situation is that many Christians do not have such a sense. The reason why they do not have any sense is that they are short of light. Do we not know that the path of life begins with confession? Even if we have decided to do a certain thing and then God shines on us, we should not do it; rather, we should confess our sins. After confessing, we will know what sin is.

There is an employee of an elementary school who often used the letterhead and envelopes of the school. This is not right. However, if the school has a regulation that says that all school letterhead and envelopes are also for personal use, then he may use them, but if there is no such regulation, it is unrighteous for him to use them. Some elementary school teachers take chalk home for their children to play with, without any sense of sin. We cannot say that this kind of person is unsaved, but we can say that he does not have the sense of sin. A person who has confessed his sins before God will not be careless in any matter. Before one confesses, he may go to other people's homes and read their newspaper or open their letters. But after his confession, he will have a sense of unrighteousness when he does the same thing. This is not merely a matter of regulation but a matter of righteousness. When we have this kind of sense we will know what is the path of Christ. If we want to grow in life, we have to confess our sins. The path of life begins with confession. Many people have heard many doctrines, but they have never taken a step on the path of life; hence, they do not have the discipline of the Holy Spirit or the restriction of the Holy Spirit. Although they do not commit great errors, they have committed many tiny mistakes. We have to look to God for His mercy, seek His shining, and confess to Him so that our sins might be forgiven.

CHAPTER FIVE

CONSECRATING OURSELVES TO THE LORD

CONFESSING SINS, DEALING WITH SINS, AND CONSECRATING OURSELVES TO THE LORD

If a Christian wants to grow in life, two things are essential: He must confess his sins thoroughly to the Lord and deal with his sins. A third thing which is equally important is consecration; he must consecrate himself absolutely to the Lord. As a basic requirement, every Christian should consecrate himself to the Lord. After a person is saved, if he desires to grow in life, he must confess and deal with his sins. The confession of sins focuses on what is on the inside while dealing with sins focuses on what is on the outside. To confess sins is to tell God the condition of one's heart and to confess to God all the sins that one feels inwardly. To deal with sins is something related to outward behavior; it involves thoroughly dealing with everything in one's living, surroundings, and home that is not pleasing to God. This is a dealing that is not only before God but also before men. The inward confession of sins plus the outward dealing with sins—the two combined together—are a complete experience.

However, after a person is saved, if he merely confesses his sins before God and deals with his sins before men but does not consecrate himself to God, he has not yet started to walk on the path of life. We have to know that after a person's salvation, the first step always includes confession of sins, dealing with sins, and consecration to the Lord. In our experience, these three things may be in a different sequence. Some may confess their sins first and then consecrate themselves to the Lord; some may consecrate themselves to the Lord first and then deal with their sins. The order does not matter.

After a person is saved, the first step always includes these three things: a thorough confession of his sins before God, a careful dealing with his sins before men, and the consecration of himself to the Lord. These three things combined together are a complete experience.

This can be likened to our breakfast. A complete Chinese breakfast is composed of bread, porridge, and some small dishes of food. It does not matter whether we eat the porridge, the bread, or the small dishes of food first. In the same way, after a person's salvation, his first experience should include confession of sins to God from within, a thorough dealing with sins before men, and an absolute consecration to the Lord. All these three things are equally necessary, but their sequence is not that important. It does not matter whether or not others encourage you to do these three things, because all those who are saved and desire to take the Lord's way cannot avoid them. Anyone who has not experienced these few matters has never taken a step before the Lord. Even if some have experienced only the first matter, only the second matter, or both matters, if they have not experienced the third matter, they still have not yet taken a complete step before the Lord.

We have to ask the Lord to show us where we really are. Regardless of whether we have a definite heart to take the Lord's way or we have just a little determination, we must realize that there is no short cut in the spiritual path. When we leave the house, we have to first pass through the front door before we get to the gate. In the same way, there are certain sections in the Lord's way, and we cannot skip any step. We may listen to messages and read the Bible, but if we do not have a heart to take the Lord's way, messages will not help us, and reading the Bible will not be beneficial to us. Messages should render much help to people, and reading the Bible should supply them with life, but if we merely understand the Lord's way and do not have a heart, then nothing will be profitable to us. We should not be those who merely understand the Lord's way; we should be those who also have a heart. Not only so, we should not merely have a heart, we also should begin to walk on the way. If so, every single message we hear will be profitable to us, and every verse of the

Bible that we read will be a supply to us. I hope that every one of us would be one who has a heart and walks on the way.

GOD REQUIRING MAN TO BELIEVE IN HIM AND TO LOVE HIM

Thus, we can see that in addition to confessing and dealing with our sins, consecrating ourselves to the Lord is of great importance. There are two crucial points in the entire Bible. First, God requires man to believe in Him, and second, God requires man to love Him. None of the leaders of the world require man to believe in them or to love them. Neither Mohammed nor Confucius ever asked anyone to believe in him or to love him. Only Jesus Christ wants man to believe in Him and to love Him.

Since man's fall, God's demand on man has been first, faith and second, love. Do you know what it means to be saved? To be saved is to turn to God, that is, to believe in God and to have a relationship with God. When a person does not have God, he is alienated from God; regardless of whether this alienation is great or small, he is alienated and severed from God. How are we united to God and joined to God? This happens through faith. The more we believe, the more we are joined to God; the more we believe, the more we are united with God and the stronger our contact with God is. Many people say that there is no God, because they use the wrong organ to try to contact God. For instance, if we use our ears to try to hear colors, we surely will not be able to hear anything; if we use our eyes to see smell, we surely will not be able to see anything. The more we believe in God, the more we realize His existence; and the more we believe in Him, the more we sense His presence. The relationship that man has with God is one of faith.

Second, the relationship that man has with God is characterized by love. It is wonderful that after man believes in Him, what He requires of man is love. Every saved one, everyone who believes in God, has the feeling within him that the Lord is lovely. If we ask someone who worships Buddha whether Buddha is lovely or not, he will say that he has never thought about this. If we ask someone who believes in the

Lord, regardless of how much love he has, he at least has some feeling that he loves the Lord; he at least has some heart to do something for the Lord. Hence, as long as a person is saved, without anyone teaching him, he spontaneously has a feeling within him that the Lord is lovely and that he wants to love the Lord.

ALL THE SAVED ONES FEELING
THAT THE LORD IS LOVELY

Although some saved ones may not feel very strongly that the Lord is lovely or that they want to love God, within them they still have a little love for the Lord. One time I went to visit a brother who loved playing cards. I asked him, "Which do you think is more lovely—the Lord or the cards?" He said, "Outwardly I feel that the cards are more lovely, but inwardly I still feel that the Lord is more lovely." In fact, he knew that it was a good thing for him to love the Lord, yet he still enjoyed playing cards. These two things were competing for this person—the Lord was competing from within while the cards were competing from without. One day, however, the cards will lose, and the Lord will gain the victory. Sooner or later the power inside of him will overcome the power which is outside of him. A person who hates sins does not do so because he is afraid of sins. Christians hate sins because the Lord is lovely and they have the Lord's love within them.

Every saved one inwardly feels that the Lord is lovely. It is not a matter of "knowing," because knowing is just a matter of our mind; rather, it is a matter of "feeling." Feeling is a matter of an inner sense. A saved one not only knows that the Lord is lovely, but he also feels that the Lord is lovely. A Christian may commit a great sin. While committing the sin, he may, on the one hand, enjoy the pleasures of sin while, on the other hand, still feel that the Lord is lovely. Hence, a Christian is almost always a paradox. Nearly every Christian is different on the inside than he is on the outside and experiences contradictions between what he is within and what he is without. It is rare to find a Christian whose inner being is in harmony with his outer being. What is it to have one's inner being in harmony with one's outer being? This is to love the Lord without and within. The majority of Christians love themselves outwardly, but inwardly they still love the Lord. Some love to dress up outwardly, but inwardly they still love the Lord. Some love their wife outwardly, but inwardly they still love the Lord. Some love their children outwardly, but inwardly they still love the Lord. Every Christian more or less loves the Lord. On the one hand, we do like lustful things, fashion, and clothing, but on the other hand, we feel that the Lord is truly lovely.

Although there may be a difference in degree, every Christian does feel that the Lord is lovely. This is the motivation of a Christian's consecration. After we are saved, the Lord draws our heart to Himself over and over again in many ways and through different kinds of environments and methods, so that we would tell Him, "O Lord, not only do You love me but You are truly lovely. I fully consecrate myself to You." All Christians have to take this initial step, and no one can escape from this. Anyone who has never given himself to the Lord has no way to take the Lord's way.

CONSECRATION BEING
THE BEGINNING OF ALL EXPERIENCES

After someone is saved, if he wants to have a rich experience of the Lord, the first step he needs to take is consecration. If a person does not give himself to the Lord after his salvation, he will have no way to take the Lord's way. For our prayers to be answered, faith is of vital importance; however, those who have never given themselves to the Lord cannot have much faith. Only those who truly consecrate themselves to the Lord have adequate faith. After we have absolutely consecrated ourselves to the Lord, faith comes. Faith comes from consecration. Moreover, if a person desires to belong to the Lord completely, he must fully consecrate himself to the Lord. No one can be holy without consecrating himself to the Lord. A person will have no way to overcome if he has not consecrated himself to the Lord. Furthermore, one can see hardly any light unless he consecrates himself to the Lord. How well we walk before God altogether hinges on our consecration. Man's heart always turns to the world, but only when man turns to God will God shine on him with His light.

Suppose there is a light behind me. If I do not turn around, I will not receive its shining because light shines in a particular direction. When a man's heart is turned to things other than God, it is impossible for God to shine on him. Some pray that God would shine on them, but still they do not receive any light. Some may even wonder why others always receive light, but they never receive any light. This is solely because they are turned away from God. Whenever they turn around, God's light will have a way to shine on them. "Whenever their heart turns to the Lord, the veil is taken away" (2 Cor. 3:16). If a Christian does not have light within him, this shows that inwardly he is still somewhat turned away from God. Since he is turned away from God, he needs to turn around. What is consecration? Consecration is to turn our whole being around. When our heart is in the world, we spontaneously are facing the world; hence, we need to turn. Whenever our heart is facing the Lord within, immediately our inner being will be enlightened, and we will know what is the will of God and what is not the will of God.

Moreover, for a Christian to be spiritual, he also must consecrate himself to the Lord. We may use an illustration: A cup can be placed outside for half a day while the rain is very heavy, but the cup is not filled with even half a drop of water. Why not? The reason the cup is not filled up is because it is upside down. Although the rain is pouring down, the cup does not have one drop of water. All children of God should be filled with the Holy Spirit, and it should be easy for them to receive the filling of the Holy Spirit. However, some people always ask for the filling of the Holy Spirit yet never receive it. What is the reason for this? If we turn the cup right side up, it will be filled with water right away. If we are not willing to turn our heart to face toward God but instead are always facing "downward," facing toward the world, then it is impossible for us to be filled with the Holy Spirit. It is absolutely impossible for a person whose heart is totally toward the world to be filled with the Holy Spirit and to receive the grace of God. However, as soon as he turns his heart toward God, he will immediately be filled with the Holy Spirit. All the experienced ones can testify of this. Furthermore, a person also must be consecrated if he wants to fellowship with God and have His presence all the time. Anyone who is not consecrated cannot have fellowship with God; neither can he have the presence of God. We can use an electric lamp as an illustration. If an electric lamp has a broken wire, the electricity is cut off. In this case, having one broken wire is the same as having two broken wires. Therefore, for us to enjoy the fellowship and the presence of God, we must be consecrated people.

THE GRACE AND BLESSING OF GOD COMING UPON THE CONSECRATED ONES

To love God and to believe in God are equally important. We must believe in Him and love Him; then His grace, His blessing, and His presence will come upon us. For the grace of God, the blessing of God, and the presence of God to come upon us, we have to love Him. Of course, those who do not believe in God would not love God; for one to love, he first has to believe. If we love Him, we will turn to Him. We always hear people say that we have to wait for God; in fact, this is not correct. It is not we who wait for God, but it is God who waits for us. God is waiting for us to turn to Him so that He can answer our prayers and give us power. It is not we who wait for God, but it is God who is waiting for us. As we have illustrated before, the rain outside may be heavy, but if the cup is facing downward, how can we expect the rainwater to enter into the cup? If a person is not willing to turn to God, how can the grace of God come upon such a one? God is always waiting for us to turn from the earth to the heavens. Thus, it is not man who waits for God's grace, but it is God who is waiting for man to receive Him as grace day by day.

Here is the problem: It is not that easy for man's heart to turn to God. Only those who have been touched by the Lord's love can easily receive the grace of God. Those who do not have faith will easily obtain faith after they have consecrated themselves to the Lord. Those who do not have holiness will easily obtain holiness after consecration. Those who do not have light will easily obtain light after consecration. Those

who do not have the presence of God will have the presence of
God after consecration. Those who do not have power will
have power in their daily lives after consecration. Everything
depends upon whether or not we have our heart turned to the
Lord. If our heart is turned to the Lord, then the Lord Himself, the grace of the Lord, spiritual light, and spiritual riches
will all be poured into us. But if our heart is not turned to the
Lord, even if the Lord grants us grace, there is no way for
grace to enter into us, just as the rainwater cannot enter into
the cup.

What is consecration? Consecration is to turn to God. Formerly, we wanted something apart from God, but now we are
encouraged by the Lord's love from within, we turn to God,
and we want only God Himself. Whoever turns to God in this
way easily touches God and receives God's grace. If we are
willing to give ourselves to God like this, when we pray,
our prayer will become very special; when we read the Bible,
the Bible will become full of light to us; when we preach the
gospel, our gospel preaching will become very powerful. A
Christian should thoroughly consecrate himself to the Lord at
least once, if not several times. Then, if after a period of time
he feels that his past consecration was not thorough enough,
he should consecrate himself thoroughly a second time. After
some more time he may even feel that his second consecration
was not thorough enough. Then he should consecrate himself
to the Lord once again. Even after a further period of time, he
may consecrate himself absolutely to the Lord once again.
The more he consecrates to the Lord like this, the more he
will touch the Lord and the more he will be gained by the
Lord. A person like this will walk on the Lord's way and grow
in life every day.

ABSOLUTELY OBEYING THE INNER FEELING
AFTER CONSECRATION

After we have consecrated ourselves to the Lord, we have
to follow the Lord's feeling absolutely. After we have consecrated ourselves to the Lord, our inner being is enlightened.
As a result, we will know what pleases the Lord and we will
follow our inner feeling. Romans 12:1 says that we should

present our bodies a living sacrifice to God. If we present ourselves to God in this way, the result will be that we know the well pleasing and perfect will of God. God will let us know what is pleasing to Him, and He will also let us know what is not pleasing to Him. When He does this, we have to obey every single feeling within us absolutely. If a Christian merely listens to doctrines and exhortations without practicing to follow the Lord's inner leading and without walking on the Lord's way, his listening does not mean anything. The most precious thing about a Christian is that after he has consecrated himself to the Lord, he is able to sense what is pleasing to the Lord, what is not pleasing to Him, and is able to live according to that feeling. This is the most valuable thing in the Christian experience.

There was once a sister who was very fashionable. One day she gave herself to the Lord and said, "O Lord, from now on, I consecrate myself to You. I do not want anything apart from You; whether I can live this way or not, I do not care. I just give myself to You." Two or three days after she prayed, she wore a very fashionable dress to the meeting. No one had ever told her that she should not wear that dress, and she had never read in the Bible that she should not wear such a dress. Nevertheless, after her consecration when she had taken the dress out of her closet, within her she felt that she should not. She did not understand, so she stood there awhile analyzing whether or not it is sinful to wear such a dress. Then she took the dress out of the closet, and the uncomfortable feeling remained within her. After she put the dress on, she felt even more uncomfortable. Then she reasoned with herself that in the past when she attended the Lord's Day meeting, the preacher never told her that she was not allowed to wear that dress. Eventually, she left the house wearing the dress.

After she left the house, she had the feeling that she should go back into the house, but she still did not understand why. While she was walking, her inner being was arguing with her, "You could wear this dress in the past but not today. Other people can wear this dress but not you." She really did not have the peace within. When she arrived at the entrance of the meeting hall, the urging within her to go

home made her very uncomfortable. She had no way to deal
with this pressing feeling, so at the very moment when she
was crossing the threshold of the meeting hall, she withdrew
and went back home. When she went home, she was totally
released because her inner being was in harmony with her
outer man. After she came back to the meeting hall in another
dress, the meeting that day was enjoyable to her in an unpre-
cedented way. That day she learned the lesson that man can
truly live before God and in fellowship with Him.

How far a person will walk on the Lord's way depends
entirely on how much he lives before God. Once our heart
turns to God, we will immediately have God's feeling and
know what is of God and what is not of God. This kind of
experience is only given to those who are walking on God's
way. This kind of living is not according to the natural human
life, but according to the life within.

There is a sister who once went to buy some fabric. In the
fabric shop she saw a piece of wool fabric. She wanted to buy
it, but her inner being told her not to buy it but instead to
send the money to a certain place to help with the Lord's
work there. After she considered for awhile, she bought the
fabric. After she went home, she felt very unpeaceful for three
days. After three days she told a brother about this matter.
She told him, "I bought a piece of fabric, but in the end I actually bought a sin." That brother just happened to be in need
of some fabric, so he asked her to resell it to him. Then this
sister followed her inner feeling and offered the money that
she received from selling the fabric to the Lord's work.

We have to obey the inner feeling. Otherwise, sooner or
later we have to confess this sin of disobedience, just like that
sister did. This shows us that one who walks on God's way,
must, at a minimum, take care of a few matters: to thoroughly confess all his sins before God, to clearly deal with all
his sins before the world, and to entirely consecrate himself to
the Lord. By doing this, he will have the Lord's presence
within, and he will be able to have fellowship with the Lord
and to have the Lord's feeling. Once he has the Lord's feeling,
he should obey every feeling that he receives from the Lord.
The more he obeys these feelings, the more sensitive his inner

being will become. May the Lord have mercy on us. May He save each one of us from being one who merely listens to doctrines and cause us to be those who walk on His way with a turned heart.

CHAPTER SIX

DEALING WITH THE CONSCIENCE

Acts 24:16 says, "Because of this I also exercise myself to always have a conscience without offense toward God and men." Second Timothy 1:3a also mentions, "I thank God, whom I serve from my forefathers in a pure conscience." Acts speaks of "a conscience without offense," while 2 Timothy speaks of "a pure conscience." Moreover, 1 Timothy 1:19 says, "Holding faith and a good conscience, concerning which some, thrusting these away, have become shipwrecked regarding the faith." Verse 2 of chapter four mentions, "By means of the hypocrisy of men who speak lies, of men who are branded in their own conscience as with a hot iron." Ephesians 4:19 also says, "Who, being past feeling [conscience], have given themselves over to lasciviousness to work all uncleanness in greediness." These verses show us the importance of the conscience in a Christian's living.

A Christian who wants to grow in life must do three things: first, thoroughly confess his sins before God; second, carefully deal with his sins before man; and third, consecrate himself to God absolutely. If the saints are willing to take these three things to the Lord and practice them in a serious way, they surely will have progress in life. However, if they only take these words as doctrines, they will not receive much help from them. These words are only guidelines; only when the saints seriously walk the way of the Lord will these words be profitable to them. The experience of these three matters—confessing our sins to God, confessing our mistakes to man, and consecrating ourselves absolutely to God—may vary in sequence. These three matters are like a threefold cord, and no one who takes the Lord's way can neglect them.

Moreover, after a Christian has thoroughly confessed his sins, carefully dealt with them, and consecrated himself to God, he also has to deal with his conscience. This is the necessary pathway for a Christian to take. After we confess our sins before God, deal with our sins before man, and consecrate ourselves to God, we will immediately have a feeling deep within us. This feeling is not merely a realization in our mind, but a feeling in the depths of our being that we have to deal with our conscience and obtain peace in our conscience. Therefore, it is extremely important to know the origin, the position, and the function of the conscience.

THE ORIGIN, POSITION, AND FUNCTION
OF THE CONSCIENCE

In simple words, the conscience comes from God. People who know God should know that before the fall of Adam, man lived before God and had no need of the conscience. For example, when we are in the sunlight during the day, there is no need of a lamp or any other kind of light. Only those who are not facing the sun have the need of a light. The need of the conscience arose as a result of the fall, when man left the face of God. In the beginning man lived before God, who can be likened to the sun. Originally man received light directly from the face of God. Although candlelight is weak, it is not without function; when the sun has set, the candlelight starts to function. It is the same with the function of the conscience. When man was living before God and had the light of God, the conscience was not used and the function of the conscience was not expressed because man had no need of it before God. We see from human history that man fell not long after he was created. He fell from light into darkness. After the fall there was a distance, a barrier, between God and man. At that point the Bible shows us that God took the definite step to activate the function of man's conscience. This may be likened to lighting a lamp when the sky is getting dark. We have to bear in mind that the function of the conscience was activated after man's fall.

The position of the conscience is to represent, or we can say, stand in the place of, God inside of man. Thus, although living according to the conscience is good, it is not the highest condition. The highest condition is that man would live before God directly. Why do we need a lamp? We need a lamp because the sky is dark. Why do we need the conscience? We need the conscience because man is fallen. Since man fell and left the face of God, God was forced to use the conscience as His representative in enlightening man. Human history can be divided into several dispensations. The first dispensation is called the dispensation of innocence; it is the time when man received direct ruling from God. After the fall the second dispensation, the dispensation of conscience, began. At that time man had both sin and a conscience within him. Although man had fallen into the darkness of sin, God still preserved a conscience, a lamp, for man. The conscience of man was still able to enlighten man and manifest its function. This was how the conscience was activated.

THE FALL OF MAN

Man's fall was not a partial fall but a complete fall, and a continual fall. Man did not stay under the ruling of the conscience but he continued to fall. How did man fall further? We see from human history that man's fall into sin was progressive. First, man fell into the conscience, and it was the conscience which enlightened and ruled over man. Yet man was not able to stand firm under the ruling of the conscience, and so from there he fell again. After the first step of man's fall, man had the conscience within him which represented God to rule over man. Yet man ignored his conscience in everything he did and fell again. At this time the dispensation of law began, and man started to be penalized if he disobeyed the laws of the nation. At this juncture man had fallen to the uttermost.

Man is really strange: The more he is ruled by man, the further he falls. For instance, a person who is always supervised by his parents will do improper things once his parents are not supervising him. A student will also do something against the rules when he is not under school regulations. If there were no police in a nation or a society, the whole nation would be full of crime. This is why many robbers and bandits fear neither heaven nor earth, but they fear the laws of the nation. If they have a way to escape from the law, they will do many evil things. This proves that man is utterly fallen.

We have no way to really categorize man. If we have to do so, we may simply divide man into three categories. The first category is the highest, but there are very few people in it. This category of people lives directly before God. These people are full of light and are like the shining of the sun. However, the number of people in this category is extremely small. Those in this category are Christians who are very spiritual and very holy.

The second category of people is also composed of Christians and is also small. This category comprises those who live by their conscience and have a very keen conscience. The children in this category do not require the supervision of their parents; the students do not require the regulation of their schools; and the common people are law-abiding people who do not require the ruling of the police. This group of people lives under the ruling of the conscience. They do not require the ruling of man because their conscience enlightens and regulates them. Anything that they sense is improper, they would not do. No law can completely rule over man, but the ruling of the conscience far exceeds the ruling of the law. This is the second category of people—those who live under the ruling of the conscience.

The third category of people is neither governed by God nor by their conscience. The people in this category do not fear the laws of the nation or the regulations of their families. They are able to do all kinds of evil things.

Another category of people, between the first and the second categories, is composed of those who live according to their conscience and, at the same time, are learning to live before God. These are advancing Christians. A normal and progressing Christian lives not only by his conscience, but also before God.

In the fall, man fell from the face of God to the conscience and from the conscience to the law. We all, more or less, also have this kind of experience. When we were young, our parents charged us not to steal any candy. If we did, our heart would beat very heavily. When we stole some candy a second time, our heart beat less heavily. When we stole candy a third time, our heart beat even less. Then the fourth time we stole candy, our heart did not beat any heavier than normal because our conscience did not have any more feeling. The fifth time that we stole, we did not fear anything except being caught by our parents. At that point it seemed that to steal candy was nothing; the only thing we feared was being caught by our parents. Similarly, the first time we cheated on an examination in school our heart beat very heavily; then the second time our heart beat less heavily; the third time our heart beat even softer; and the fourth time our heart did not beat any more than normal. As long as we were not caught by our teachers, everything was fine. What does this illustrate? This illustrates how we have fallen from the ruling of the conscience to the ruling of man.

Moreover, immoral relationships between males and females are also the same. The first time when people do something immoral, they do have some feeling in their conscience; the second time they have less feeling; the third time they have even less feeling; by the fourth time they do not have any feeling at all. The fifth time they fear very little; they fear only the laws of the nation, or they fear being seen by man. This is the fall of man from the feeling of the conscience to the ruling of man. Robbers and thieves are the same all over the world; if there were no police or government, the chaos of the world would be beyond our imagination.

Most lawless people fear the penalty of the laws of the nation. Our Lord is saving us from living in this way. After our salvation if we still do things against our family's rules, against school regulations, or against the laws in society, then I am afraid that we are not truly saved, or that if we are saved, we do not look like Christians. God saves us out of the lowest point of the fall. An unsaved person makes a mess in his family, in society, and in the nation; this is the fall of man. A saved person does not require the control of his parents at home because he is already an obedient child; he does not require the supervision of the school because he is already a regulated student; he also does not require the governing of society or the nation because he is already a good man, a law-abiding citizen. He abides by the laws not because he fears the laws, but because he is living by his conscience. In the fall, man fell from the face of God to the conscience and from the conscience to human rule. Human rule is the lowest point of man's fall, the place where God's salvation reaches man.

THE SALVATION OF GOD

The lowest point of the fall is that man has to be ruled by other people. If a wife has to be ruled by her husband, a husband has to be ruled by his wife, and the children have to be ruled by their parents, then this proves that they are fallen to the uttermost. Some people work in an organization or a company which stipulates that its employees should come to work at eight o'clock, but every day they try to find out whether or not the manager will be coming to work at eight o'clock the next morning. If he will be coming to work at eight o'clock, they also will come to work at eight o'clock; however, if the manager has to go somewhere and will not come in until eight-thirty, they will come in at eight-thirty as well. Should a Christian do such a thing? If there are some among us who do such a thing, this does not mean that they are not saved, but at least we can say that they do not live before their conscience. A saved person goes to work at eight o'clock when his manager comes at eight, but when his manager does not come at eight o'clock, he still goes to work at eight. He lives this way because God has already saved him from living by human rule and has caused him to live by his conscience. Many people are truly saved, but sadly, many Christian wives still deceive their husbands and tell lies in front of their children. This is not the proper manner and conduct of a Christian. If a Christian is thoroughly saved, he should be saved from this kind of condition.

Ten years ago I was serving in a certain locality. One day a brother came to me and said, "I have a problem that I have been unable to solve for a few days. Please help me." Then I asked him what the matter was, and he replied, "I was saved a long time ago, but later I became backslidden. Not only did

I play cards all the time, but I also stole electricity from the electric company. At that time many people did such a thing, and I did it almost every day. But now by God's mercy, I am revived, and whenever I think of those days of stealing electricity, I feel very uncomfortable. I do not know what to do." Please notice that formerly this person did not fear anybody; he feared neither heaven nor earth but only the meter man from the electric company. He feared man but did not fear his conscience. One day, however, he was revived to the extent that he sensed that his conscience was not at peace. As a result, he could not steal electricity anymore, and he felt that he had to make payment for all the electricity that he had stolen in the past. When he came to me, he was in this difficult situation. I told him, "It is very simple. You just need to estimate a rough amount of all the electricity that you have stolen in the past and then pay it back to the electric company." He said, "This is really difficult. First of all, it is hard to calculate the amount accurately, and second, I do not have the face and the courage to do so." Then I told him, "It is not too hard. First, you just calculate an approximate amount and then add a little more; as long as your conscience does not condemn you, then this is good enough. Second, even though it is a shame to do this, at the same time, it is something glorious because it pleases God when someone repents and regrets what he has done in the past."

The brother thought about my word and found it reasonable. Then he went back and calculated the amount, signed a check, wrote a sincere letter, and told the electric company the whole story. He wrote, "I stole electricity from your company in the past, but now I have become a Christian. I have an unpeaceful feeling in my conscience telling me that I should repay you, or I will remain unpeaceful." Shortly after this, a brother who ran an electronics store went to the electric company to talk with someone concerning a few matters. The head accountant saw this brother and said to him, "Please help me to see if this check that I received is real or fake. Is this person a mental case?" The brother answered, "I know this person; he is not a mental case." Then the brother testified to the accountant what had happened, and the head accountant was deeply touched when he heard it.

There was once a sister who used to be very careless. In 1932, after she was revived by God, she immediately began to live by her conscience. Through the feeling of her conscience, she realized that some years ago she had committed a disgraceful act. At that time traveling from Nanking to Shanghai was very convenient; there was a direct train that went back and forth between the two cities. This train, however, required a ticket. This sister had studied in America and was a professor at a university. She was also a responsible person among the female students. Many people who worked for the Railway Administration knew her, and they helped her to get an employee pass, which enabled her to ride the train for free. Even a person who had graduated from a university, who had studied abroad, and who was a university professor could do such a poor thing and could behave like a thief and covet such a small benefit. Most rebellious and lawless people first disobey God, then disregard their conscience, and third, defy the law. Hence, when they defy the law, this indicates that they have already disobeyed God and disregarded their conscience. At this stage, as long as they are not penalized by the law, they are able to do anything. This is the condition of fallen man.

However, after this sister was saved, her conscience immediately enlightened her and gave her the feeling that she had done something unrighteous and that she owed the government for using the employee pass. She felt very unpeaceful, so she went to fellowship with the saints. The saints told her that she should calculate the amount that she owed and deal with it carefully. She said that it was not a problem to pay the money back, but she did not know how to calculate the amount or how to return the money. At that time the income of the Nanking-Shanghai Railway went to the national treasury. In light of this, everyone suggested that after she had calculated the amount, she should send the money directly to the Minister of Finance, because if the money had to be transferred from the people at the lower levels, it would easily be lost. Therefore, she wrote a letter to the Minister of Finance and sent the money to him. Later, the Nanking newspaper printed this story.

DEALING WITH THE CONSCIENCE

Every saved one has to deal with his conscience. If he does not deal with his conscience, he will not have peace within. If he does not deal with his conscience, he will not be able to pray properly. If he does not deal with his conscience, his Bible reading will be tasteless and his gospel preaching will be powerless. If he does not deal with his conscience, he will not be able to walk the pathway ahead of him. All the saved ones have to pass through this stage of dealing with their conscience if they want to go further on the way. Our conscience is like a window and our being is like a room; the light that the room (our being) receives must pass through the window (our conscience). Originally, there is no light inside of us but only darkness, but our conscience is like a window which allows the light to come in.

Before we are saved, our conscience is like an extremely dirty window smudged with putty through which no light can penetrate. This results in a state of complete darkness in our being. However, once we are saved, the Holy Spirit enters into us to enlighten us, causing our inner being to be full of light. At this time, we immediately feel that we are wrong. Then we should repent and confess our sins before God, and we should deal with our sins before man. Every time we confess or deal with a sin, we wipe the putty-covered window once. The wonderful thing is that before we wipe the window, we do not know how dirty it is; so the more we wipe it, the dirtier it seems to become. Once we wipe the window even slightly, all the greasy dirt is stirred up. Then when the sunlight shines through the window, it seems even dirtier than before. However, in the end, the window will be clean.

It is the same with our conscience. When we were first saved, we may have thought that we had committed only a few small mistakes before God, but after we began to confess these mistakes, we immediately saw many greater sins. Eventually, the more we deal with our sins, the fewer sins we have. This is like wiping a window: The more we wipe it, the less greasy dirt it has. As a result of this process, we have peace within, and spontaneously we can easily pray to God. When the rain splashes mud or sand onto a dirty window, we can hardly see anything inside the house; however, after the window has been cleaned, when a little bit of sand or mud is splashed onto the window, we will notice it immediately. Many people have done something wrong yet never sense that they are wrong. This proves that they have never dealt with their conscience.

CONSCIENCE AND FAITH PROCEEDING TOGETHER

One who desires to proceed on the path of God's life must deal with his conscience, because conscience and faith go together. When we pray, we need to have faith. Prayer without faith equals not praying at all. God listens only to the prayers of faith, and He will not listen to any prayers which are not out of faith. However, once we have a problem with our conscience, faith is gone, and once there is a hole in our conscience, faith leaks away. We can still pray and plead, yet if we do not have faith and our conscience does not have any feeling, we will be like a tire with a hole in it—the more air we pump into it, the more air it leaks out and the flatter it becomes. First Timothy 1:19 says, "Holding faith and a good conscience, concerning which some, thrusting these away, have become shipwrecked regarding the faith." The trend of society toward corruption is not something that was there in the beginning. It was not this way in the past. Today even the academic circles are full of lies. Teachers cheat their students, and students deceive their parents. Every place is full of lies. This is the case among the young people in particular. Even young people who are Christians tell lies both at home and in school. They think that it is very difficult not to tell lies. This is the reason why they have no progress in the faith.

If we have a feeling when we tell a lie for the first time, we should carefully deal with it and not allow it to pass away. If we tell a lie to someone and do not have peace in our conscience, we have to go to that person and deal with it immediately, saying, "I am sorry. The thing that I just said to you is a lie; it is not true." In this way our inner being will be full of light. Perhaps we will be full of light for three days.

Then we may encounter another incident and tell another lie. As soon as this happens, we should deal with the feeling that we receive from our conscience right away. If we do not, then after three or four experiences like this, the feeling in our conscience gradually will be lost. Once the feeling of our conscience is lost, not only will we tell more lies, but we will also do worse things and become shipwrecked regarding the faith.

Therefore, I am afraid that many Christians' consciences are not able to withstand the test. A preacher once told me about something that he saw one time when he went to visit a pastor. When they sat down, the pastor's child came and told his father that someone was looking for him. Then the pastor told his child in front of the preacher, "Tell him that I am not home." This shows us how very easy it is to tell a lie because a lie settles everything. However, once we tell a lie, inwardly our conscience is branded, as if with a hot iron. If we do this again and again, we will have no further feeling in our conscience; our conscience will become deadened. The conscience of many people is not a living conscience but a deadened conscience because telling lies has become their habit. A Christian will not be able to genuinely pray after he has lied, neither will he be able to genuinely pray after he has lost his temper. Some people say that they have seen Christians who have lost their temper but were able to pray immediately afterwards. There are people like this, but God never listens to the prayers of one whose conscience is numb. If a person does not listen to the voice of his conscience, neither will God listen to that person's voice. Those who do not have any feeling in their conscience certainly do not have faith in their prayers. God does not listen to the prayer of a liar. Once a person's conscience is corrupted, leaking, or numb, he will no longer be able to understand the feeling of his conscience, and God will not listen to the prayer of this kind of person.

ALWAYS HAVING A CONSCIENCE WITHOUT OFFENSE TOWARD GOD AND MAN

In Acts 24:16 Paul said, "Because of this I also exercise myself to always have a conscience without offense toward God and men." A conscience without offense is one that is without holes or leakage. If we confess our sins before God and deal with our sins before man, our inner being will be without sins and our conscience will be pure. We can serve God only with a pure conscience. If we want our service to touch God, we have to serve with a pure conscience. If our conscience is not pure, not only will our prayers not be answered, but they will never touch God. Some people's conscience is like a wrecked ship. Although some have forsaken their conscience, those who are saved should not overlook even a small mistake; rather, we should deal with it thoroughly. We do not need to encourage people to be enthusiastic, because enthusiasm in blindness does not profit anything. If we want to follow God in life to walk on the way ahead of us, we must follow Him and fulfill His principles. If we want to serve and touch God, we must always have the presence of God within us, and we must be full of light and have faith all the time. In this way, light, revelation, life, and power will become our constant experiences. As long as we thoroughly deal with our conscience, we will be able to walk on this path in a straight and proper way.

CHAPTER SEVEN

LIVING ACCORDING TO THE CONSCIENCE AND LIVING BEFORE GOD

FALLEN MAN NOT BEING GOVERNED BY HIS CONSCIENCE

First Timothy 1:5 says, "But the end of the charge is love out of a pure heart and out of a good conscience and out of unfeigned faith." Verse 19 continues, "Holding faith and a good conscience, concerning which some, thrusting these away, have become shipwrecked regarding the faith." Second Timothy 1:3 also says, "I thank God, whom I serve from my forefathers in a pure conscience." Ephesians 4:19-20 mentions, "Who, being past feeling [conscience], have given themselves over to lasciviousness to work all uncleanness in greediness. But you did not so learn Christ." All these verses show us the importance of the conscience. After man's fall, God ordained that man should be governed by his conscience. Hence, if man is in a normal condition, he will take care of the feeling in his conscience. However, fallen man neither pays attention to the feeling of his conscience nor is ruled by his conscience; instead, he gives himself over to lasciviousness.

THE GRACE OF GOD STRENGTHENING MAN

After a person is saved, he has Christ's life within him. If he wants to advance in Christ's life, however, he must deal with his conscience thoroughly. If a Christian's conscience has some offense, he will not be able to have any progress in any matter. This kind of speaking may be too heavy for some people. They may think that these four matters—a thorough confession of sins before God, a careful dealing with sins before men, a complete dealing with the conscience, and an absolute consecration to God—are too difficult and seem to contradict the word of grace. On the one hand, we are told that everything depends on the grace of God and the acts of God, and that we are not required to do anything; on the other hand, we are told that we must thoroughly confess, deal with our sins, and consecrate ourselves to God. It seems that these two aspects are in conflict with one another, causing man not to know what to do. The word of grace is pleasant to the ears, full of supply, and very soothing, whereas the word of dealing seems to be too heavy, almost cruel, too hard for man to take, and beyond what man can do. Hence, man faces such a dilemma.

In fact, the grace of God does not weaken man but strengthens man. The fact that a Christian does not thoroughly confess his sins before God or completely deal with his sins before men proves that he lacks grace. A car which does not start is either broken down or short of gas. When a car is in good condition and has enough gas, certainly it will run properly. In the same way, if a Christian does not thoroughly confess his sins before God, or deal with his sins before men, this proves that he is short of grace. If a Christian does not deal with his conscience properly or consecrate himself to God absolutely, this also proves that he is short of God's grace. The demand of God and the grace of God are not incompatible with one another; rather, they are complementary to one another.

RECEIVING THE GRACE OF GOD
TO FULFILL THE DEMAND OF GOD

There are many laws in the natural world which have two sides that are seemingly contradictory. Those who have studied physics should know that in this universe there are two different forces: centripetal force and centrifugal force. The reason why many things do not fall to the ground is that both centripetal force and centrifugal force are functioning together. A lamp is another example. To illuminate, a lamp requires two electrical wires; a single wire does not work. Another example is that in the universe there is not only rainwater but also sunlight. The rainwater supplies, whereas the sunlight consumes. Only when both the sunlight and the rainwater work together are all things able to grow. If the plants receive only the shining of the sun from the beginning to the end of the year, yet do not receive the watering of the rain, they will have no way to grow. Conversely, if there is only the watering of the rain without the shining of the sun, the plants will not be able to grow. Moreover, we also know that there are both night and day, so that all things can work and rest in a perfect order. In the same way, a person's growth also hinges on both supply and consumption. All doctors exhort people to eat and to exercise. Eating is for the supply, while exercising is for the consumption. The spiritual life follows the same principle.

If a Christian only receives God's grace and love without fulfilling God's demand, he definitely will not grow well. The more a Christian receives God's grace and fulfills God's demand, the better and faster he will grow. A proper Christian should be a person who, on the one hand, receives God's grace and love while, on the other hand, strictly and absolutely fulfills God's demand. When God asks him to deal with his sins, a proper Christian will unreservedly deal with them. When God asks him to confess his sins, he will confess them without reasoning. When God asks him to consecrate himself, he will completely consecrate himself to God. When God asks him to deal with his conscience, he will thoroughly deal with his conscience. A proper Christian is neither careless nor does he do things in an incomplete way; rather, he thoroughly deals with his conscience. All the experienced ones can testify that when a person has received grace before God, he will definitely confess and deal with his sins, consecrate himself to God, and deal with his conscience.

A person who confesses and deals with his sins, consecrates himself to God, and deals with his conscience will certainly receive more grace. If we exercise enough, we surely will love eating and will eat well. In the same way, the more strictly we fulfill God's demand, the stronger His grace will be within us. Seemingly, the two are contradictory to one another, but in fact they are complementary. Without the grace of God we have no way to fulfill all these demands, and if we do not fulfill the demands, we will not receive more grace. I hope that we would not misunderstand or misinterpret these words and think that there is no way for us to fulfill them. By the grace of God, we are able to fulfill God's demand; by the grace of God, we are able to deal with all sins.

EXPERIENCING THE SPECIAL GRACE OF GOD
IN DEALING WITH SINS

In my personal Christian life, I once had an unforgettable experience related to dealing with sins. This experience testifies how great the grace of God is, because it was the grace of God from within which supported my entire being. Only when I dealt with my sins did I see how immense the grace of God really is. For my whole life I will not forget this experience. The experience came six or seven years after my salvation, and it was the first time I truly dealt with my sins. At that time the Lord worked in me and revived me, causing me to pray all the time, to serve zealously, and to have a feeling to deal with sins thoroughly. One day the Lord enlightened me and reminded me of an incident that took place in my youth when I was working for a particular organization. The building of this organization had caught on fire, and everyone tried his best to steal things from the company. I also took two small things. The first thing was a very pretty ink box, made of porcelain, for writing Chinese calligraphy. I put it into my pocket when I was helping to pack the things of the company. The other item was a clothes brush, a Western product, which looked very nice. I put the ink box in my study, and all of my friends would admire it when they saw it. In addition, being able to use the Western brush to brush my clothes when I was getting dressed was very convenient. After I was saved, I did not notice any problem right away; I had only a small feeling that these two things were of a questionable origin. Then six or seven years later the Lord's grace reached me, and I realized that I had to thoroughly deal with the sin of stealing the ink box and the small brush. I could not read the Bible while looking at the stolen ink box. In addition, the bristles on the small brush were gone after being used for six or seven years. The need to deal with stealing these two items gave me two problems. The first problem was that the son of my former boss had been my classmate, and I knew him very well. How could I go and confess to him? I found this really hard to do. Another problem was that the bristles on the brush were already gone, so how could I return it to him? For several days and nights I could hardly sleep because I felt that I could not go. I struggled for one or two weeks, and the more I struggled, the harder it became. Then I asked God to give me the courage. At that time my boss had already died, so I thought I should pay for the two items instead of returning them. After I planned everything out, I went to my classmate's home one Lord's Day afternoon. I had everything prepared. It was at the end of the year, and he happened to be at home. When he saw me, he said, "I have not seen you for a long time." At that moment my face turned red, and I said to him, "I have come to ask for your forgiveness. That year when your company caught fire, I took advantage of the situation and stole this ink box from the office." He said, "That is nothing! This kind of small thing does not matter." I continued, "And a small brush too! But it has already worn out, so I want to pay you back this amount of money." He replied, "Do not worry about it! They are just small things." I asked him to understand me. Seeing how sincere I was, he really had no way to reject me. Then he asked me, "What do you have in your hand?" At that time the government did not allow the general public to print any calendars that included both the lunar and solar years, but there was a Catholic organization which published many calendars like this. This organization was established by Westerners, and the government did not interfere with their activities. Every year this organization would send some calendars to the company where I worked. All the employees in the company who were of comparatively higher positions would be given one. When my boss's son asked me what I had in my hand, I told him that I had a calendar with both the lunar and solar years in it. Then he said, "That is good! Give me the calendar and keep your money. The calendar will be the replacement for the items you stole." Of course, on the one hand, I was joyful, but on the other hand, I was sorrowful.

Although I had dealt with the sin, he had been unwilling to receive the money, and this troubled me. On my way home, I prayed, "O Lord, what should I do with the money?" Then inwardly I had an idea: "I should give this money to a beggar, not to a common beggar but to a special one—someone who was affected by the war going on in the suburbs." When I got home, it was already evening. Someone knocked at the door, and I went to answer. The person at the door said, "Sir, please have mercy on me!" I looked at him and saw that he was a beggar. He continued, "I have not eaten anything all day." I immediately asked him to come in and gave him Chinese buns, some water, and some small dishes of food. After he finished eating, I gave him some more buns. He said in an embarrassed way, "You are a kind-hearted man." I told him, "No, I am not kind. Jesus has prepared some money for you. Just take it." Then I saw him off, and when we reached the crossroad, he bowed to me sincerely and left. On my way home, I met an elderly brother. He insisted on giving me a calendar. When I got home and looked at the calendar, I found that it contained both the lunar and solar years. I said to the Lord, "O Lord, how fearful and awesome You are! You have prepared both a beggar and such a calendar for me. Surely I have received special grace from You."

When we are dealing with our sins, we have the presence of the Lord, and after we have dealt with our sins, we know more of the Lord. To deal with our sins and our conscience in such a way is not something of law but of grace. The more we know and experience grace, the more we will deal with our sins, and the more we receive grace, the more we will grow. I hope that all of us would become matured Christians, not "half-cooked" ones. This is something done not under the law but with the supply of grace. The more dealings we have, the more we are sanctified.

BEING SAVED TO LIVE
ACCORDING TO THE CONSCIENCE

In the beginning, man fell from the face of God to the conscience, and then from the conscience to human government. Hence, there are three things that rule over man: first,

God; second, the conscience; and third, man himself. Those who live before God are the highest category of people. Those who live according to their conscience are not in the highest category of people, but they are comparatively good people. Those who live under man's ruling are in the lowest category of people—they do not obey their conscience and do not live before God, but dare to do anything. There are only a few people who live before God; the majority of people live before men. Husbands are afraid of being caught by their wives, while the wives are afraid of being caught by their husbands. Children are afraid of being caught by their parents, while the parents are afraid of being caught by their children. Doctors are afraid of being caught by the nurses, while the nurses are afraid of being caught by the doctors. Everyone is afraid of being caught by another. Whenever there is no one ruling us, we can do all kinds of immoral things. All those people who are merely afraid of man—the police, the judge, or the military police—are the lowest and most fallen people. They fear only the eyes of man, but not God Himself. Christians today live before men more than they live according to their conscience. Those who live before God are ruled by God, those who live according to their conscience are ruled by their conscience, and those who live before men are ruled by man. These three ways of living—living before God, living according to one's conscience, and living before man—are called God's rule, self-rule, and man's rule, respectively.

When we were saved, God saved us from living under man's rule. Before we were saved, as long as other people—our husbands, our wives, our teachers, or our supervisors—could not see us, we would do all kinds of filthy things for our own interests. But one day the Lord saved us from sin and evil. In addition, He also saved and delivered us from living merely under man's rule. Now, if we are children, we do not violate our family rules, and as ordinary people, we definitely are law-abiding people. Why is this? It is because we are saved, and whatever our conscience does not allow us to do, we absolutely would not do. If this is not our experience, how can we say that we are the saved ones? Although we may be saved, sometimes we are like unsaved ones—those of us who are students still do lawless things behind our teachers' backs, and those of us who are wives still tell lies to our children and to our husbands. A Christian who wants to live before God should experience God's salvation at least to the extent that he lives according to his conscience.

This way is very basic. Man's fall into being under the ruling of the conscience is one small station. Following this, man fell further into being under the ruling of man. Whatever is forbidden by the conscience is actually forbidden by God, and whatever is not pleasing to the conscience is not pleasing to God. Whatever is condemned by the conscience is condemned by God, and whatever is censured by the conscience is, in fact, censured by God. After a Christian is saved, if he does not listen to his conscience nor fulfill the demands of his conscience, he will disobey God, lie to God, and have no way to receive God's grace. For the sake of the new believers, I have to say that this does not mean that he is not saved. He is definitely saved, but because he does not listen to God's word, he is not overcoming. Thus, we have to carefully obey our conscience to deal with all the things that are condemned, censured, or forbidden by it.

I am afraid that many children of God among us have a conscience that is full of offenses and leaks. For some, the conscience may be like a bucket with holes leaking out all the water that is put into it. Although we have heard many messages, when the messages pass through us, they all leak out of us. We seem to be touched and enlightened when we read the Bible, but all these things leak out of us, and we become like a car that has run out of gas. First Timothy 1:19 says that if we thrust away our good conscience, we become shipwrecked. Today many Christians have no progress in life because they do not thoroughly deal with their conscience. If they do not pay attention to this point, they will have no way to go on. However, the wonderful thing is that whenever we thoroughly deal with our conscience, we come to God. Once we come under the ruling of our conscience, we are immediately delivered from living under man's rule, and we live before God.

LIVING BEFORE GOD

Some people may ask, What does it mean to live before God? To live before God means that we receive leading and ruling directly from God. One time I met a sister who was very mature in the Lord. She had lived in Nanking for almost thirty years. At the end of the lunar year she wanted to buy something, not because she was following the world's custom, but because she had a need. She calculated that she would need a total of one hundred and twenty Chinese yuan. Since she was serving the Lord full-time without receiving any salary, she did not always have money in her hand. Then she prayed before God, "O God, I am Your maidservant, and now I tell You my problem. I do not want help from man, but if You do not give me this one hundred and twenty yuan, this will put You to shame." Shortly after this, a co-worker who lived a few provinces away from her suddenly had the feeling that this elderly sister from Nanking was in need of money. The amount that came to his mind was exactly one hundred and twenty Chinese yuan. This is a real story. He realized that the lunar new year was approaching and that if he remitted the money to her, it would arrive too late. So he sent a telegram to her. When the sister received the telegram, the amount was exactly the same as she had requested of the Lord. This is not a matter of the conscience but a matter of living before God.

The conscience deals with right and wrong. The conscience is not necessarily God's speaking to us directly, but it is His speaking to us through our conscience. When this sister prayed, how could a co-worker who lived a few provinces away know that she needed one hundred and twenty Chinese yuan? This was the result of living before God and fellowshipping with God. This co-worker was one who thoroughly dealt with his conscience and lived before God. When he was fellowshipping with God, God spoke to him directly and gave him the leading. We have to see this one thing: A person who is delivered from man's rule, lives according to his conscience, has fellowship with God, and lives directly before God transcends right and wrong. If people would come to him to present a case, he would not deal with it based merely on right and wrong; rather, he would make his judgment before God Himself. We have to know that many people may be right according to right and wrong, but nevertheless they may be wrong before God. To know this requires the feeling of our spirit.

For example, one day two quarreling brothers came to me. If I was one who was saved merely to the point of living according to my conscience, I would speak to them according to the sense of right and wrong in my conscience, saying, "Brother Huang, you are wrong," or "Brother Sun, you are wrong." But if I am one who is learning to live before God and learning to know and deal with my conscience, I will go deeper than the feeling of my conscience and judge according to my spirit, living absolutely before God. In terms of right and wrong, it may be that Brother Huang was wrong and Brother Sun was right; however, in terms of having a proper spirit, it may be that Brother Huang was right because his spirit before God was right. Someone may be wrong in terms of right and wrong, but his spirit is right before God. Conversely, someone may be right in terms of right and wrong, but his spirit is wrong before God.

You may say that this is very complicated and wonder how a person can be wrong related to right and wrong yet right related to the spirit. For instance, we always encounter situations where the husband and wife quarrel with one another. One day a sister came to me and said, "Brother, when my husband, your brother, is happy, he rises at three o'clock in the morning to pray and read the Bible. After he has been filled with the Holy Spirit, he goes out to preach the gospel. I cook for him, but he does not eat because he says that he has to fast and pray. You see, this is your brother. He is too much. You have to deal with him." All the reasons in the whole universe seem to be on the sisters' side; sisters are always right. It is true that the brother was wrong, but this sister was unkind. In terms of right and wrong she was right, but before God she was wrong. Even though she was right, since her person was wrong, she was totally wrong.

One time another sister came with her child to oppose her husband. They came to see me and said, "Brother Lee, when my child has to buy books, my husband does not give me the money, and when I have to buy food, he does not give me the money either. All he does is preach the gospel and does not care for anything else. Whether he rises early or late, all he does is pray." This sister came to demand an explanation from me, and her child also asked, "Is my father right in doing such a thing? We really cannot take it." I had nothing to say to the sister. At that moment, the brother came. Then the sister said to me, "Brother Lee, now you can ask him yourself whether or not this is the real situation." The brother just stood there speechless. He was being questioned like a criminal. His wife was acting like she was even higher than a judge, and the child was standing there watching them. All that I could do was to weep with the brother. In terms of right and wrong, the wife may have been right; however, in terms of their persons, the brother was the one who was still right. Although the wife had been saved, her flesh was very strong. What she said was right, but her person was wrong.

If we want to live before God, we have to deal with our sins carefully. There was a wife who was very gentle. One time she came to see me, without showing me that she was angry. She said that she wanted to have some fellowship with me. She told me that her husband prayed all the time and would not come home until midnight. While she was telling me this, she was very mild and did not show her anger at all. If we had not learned the matter of the conscience, we would easily have gone along with what she said. Seeing her good attitude and gentle manner, it would be easy to think that she must be one who has much learning in the Lord; actually, she was accusing her husband. Those who have some learning before the Lord would know that what they have heard is just the surface. Many times when we are before our conscience and before God, we have a feeling which goes deeper than right and wrong. Wherever the light shines, there is God's reigning, and there is also God's life. If man does not receive God's shining to live according to his conscience, it will be hard for him to learn to know life. Moreover, one day we all have to progress beyond living by our conscience and tell God, "O God, I do not want to live merely according to my conscience, I want to live before You."

CHAPTER EIGHT

WITH MEN "THIS" IS IMPOSSIBLE, BUT WITH GOD ALL THINGS ARE POSSIBLE

TWO PARABLES

There are two parables in Matthew 21 and 22 which occupy a very important place in the Bible. Chapter twenty-one speaks of the work in the vineyard, and chapter twenty-two mentions the wedding feast. The vineyard is a matter of work, while the wedding feast is a matter of enjoyment. The first parable is about God's sending His slaves to work, and the second parable is about God's calling his people to enjoy. While work requires man to pay a price, enjoyment is free. We have to fully grasp the principle of these two parables. The first parable portrays how God requires man to pay a price, to labor. God demands that man bear fruit. Yet the second parable tells us that God simply wants man to enjoy. Here, man is not required to pay any price because all things are ready. In this parable, if we say that God demands something of man, it is only to enjoy what God has prepared. In the first parable God demands something of man, while in the second parable man receives everything from God.

What do these two parables refer to? All Bible readers should realize that the first parable refers to the dispensation of law, while the second parable refers to the dispensation of grace. In the dispensation of law God dealt with man according to the law, demanding man to do everything, but in the dispensation of grace God deals with man by means of grace, desiring man to enjoy everything He has done. When God dealt with man according to the law, during the dispensation of the law, there was a particular situation with a particular result. In the following dispensation, when God deals with man according to grace, there is a different situation with a different result.

THE DISPENSATION OF LAW

In the dispensation of law God required man to labor, to have good behavior, to pay a price, and to sweat. When man was under the law of the Old Testament, God never supplied man but always demanded things of man. In Matthew 21 there is a vineyard in which much work needed to be done and in which man was required to labor. The entire vineyard required man to spend his time and pay a price. But what was the result? The result was that man did not bear fruit for God—man did not accomplish anything. It is not that the law was wrong, but that owing to the weakness and wickedness of man, man could not do anything good. Hence, the Lord shows us in the first parable that although God repeatedly asked man for fruit, He did not receive any fruit. This indicates that under the law, if man wants to satisfy God's demand by his own behavior and righteousness, the results are vain and empty, because man is unable to do it. This parable does not say that man gave too little fruit but that man did not have any fruit at all. Under the law, if man tries to fulfill God's demand, he will definitely fail to accomplish anything. Thus, the first parable is clearly referring to the dispensation of law.

THE DISPENSATION OF GRACE

The second parable refers to the dispensation of grace. The dispensation of grace is not likened to a vineyard but to a wedding feast. Do we need to pay a price when someone invites us to a wedding feast? No one needs to pay any price to attend a wedding feast. This shows us that in the dispensation of grace, God deals with man according to grace. Everything is prepared by God, and we are those who are called simply to enjoy. We have to look to God to show us the principle of grace that we may see that everything is ready and has been prepared by God. We are those who are called simply to enjoy and do not need to pay any price.

THE DIFFERENCE BETWEEN
THE LAW IN THE OLD TESTAMENT
AND GRACE IN THE NEW TESTAMENT

The law requires us to work, whereas grace requires us to receive. The law is for us to labor, while grace is for us to enjoy. There are two pictures here: one is the picture of the vineyard where everyone is laboring, and the other one is the picture of the wedding feast where everyone is enjoying. In the dispensation of law it was man who worked, labored, and toiled. In the dispensation of grace it is God who makes everything ready and prepares everything; man simply needs to enjoy.

What is the significance of these two parables? We already know that a person who wants to grow in life before God must confess his sins and deal with his sins and conscience. But some people may say that this word is too high and wonder who can do it. Or they may ask, "Who can deal with his sins and conscience so thoroughly? In the New Testament God requires us to deal with our sins, to confess our sins, to deal with our conscience, and to consecrate ourselves to Him in a thorough way. Are these requirements of the law or of grace?" If we carefully read the New Testament, we find that there are some definite places in the New Testament which require us to confess our sins and deal with our conscience. For example, Matthew 5:26 says, "You shall by no means come out from there until you pay the last quadrans." Also, Hebrews 9:14 tells us that we have to deal with our sins in order that we may serve the living God with a pure conscience. Outwardly, all these words seem to be laws, but in the New Testament all these words are actually grace.

Here is the problem. Did we not say that only the law demands things of people and that grace is all about enjoyment without any demand? Since confessing our sins, dealing with our sins, and dealing with our conscience are obviously demands, how can we say that they are related to grace? On the surface it seems that all these matters are demands, but in fact, in the New Testament everything is grace, absolutely grace. In the Old Testament we see that God spoke many demanding words to man. For instance, Deuteronomy 6:5 clearly says, "And you shall love Jehovah your God with all your heart and with all your soul and with all your might." The New Testament also has this requirement and tells us that we should leave everything to love the Lord (Luke 10:27; Matt. 19:29; Luke 14:26). These two commandments—one in the Old Testament and one in the New Testament—are apparently the same, but actually they are not.

THE LAW OF THE OLD TESTAMENT SHOWING MAN'S INABILITY

Another example is that the Old Testament requires man to honor his father and mother (Exo. 20:12), and the New Testament also requires man to honor his father and mother (Eph. 6:2-3). The Old Testament requires man to be holy (Lev. 19:2), and the New Testament also requires man to be holy (1 Pet. 1:16). It seems that the Old Testament and the New Testament are saying the same thing, and it is hard to tell the difference. It is true that the commandments of both the Old and the New Testament are words which proceed out of the mouth of God, but the holiness in the Old Testament is truly different from that in the New Testament. In brief, all the commandments of the Old Testament are to prove the inability and incapability of man. In the Old Testament time God gave the commandments and decreed the law for man to obey and follow, but in doing this He had only one purpose—to show that man is incapable and incompetent.

Have we ever considered why in the Old Testament God wanted man to honor his parents, to be holy, to love Him, and so forth? Did God give the law for man to violate or to keep? All those who know the Bible understand that there is no way for man to keep the law of God. If so, why did God still decree the law? We need to pay attention to this one thing. Because man did not know himself, God gave him a very strict demand so that he would know himself. God seemed to be saying, "You are seriously ill and need rest, but since you are not willing to do so, I have no choice but to send you to work in the vineyard so that you may know your true condition."

The problem is that until now many of us still do not know ourselves. God, however, knows man completely and thoroughly. Man has no way to please God, and none of man's good behavior can meet God's requirements or be acceptable to God. Yet man still thinks that he is very capable and can do everything. It is in this situation that God gives man the law and demands that man be holy and love Him absolutely. Since man is unable to fulfill any of the law, eventually man's inability is exposed.

When God gave man the law in the Old Testament, He never expected man to keep the law because He already knew that man would not be able to do so. The only purpose of the law is to prove man's incapability. All the laws of the Old Testament are used to show man's inability and incompetence. Hence, whenever we read a commandment or a law, we should prostrate ourselves before God and say, "O God, I cannot do it. You want me to love You from my whole heart, with my whole soul, my whole mind, and my whole strength, but I cannot even give you one, let alone four, of these 'wholes.'" This kind of realization is exactly what God is after.

Luke 10:27 says, "You shall love the Lord your God from your whole heart and with your whole soul and with your whole strength and with your whole mind, and your neighbor as yourself." In the Bible the demand for love has two sides: four "wholes" toward God—*whole* heart, *whole* soul, *whole* strength, and *whole* mind—and one "as" toward man—love your neighbor *as* yourself. If we ask ourselves, do we have any of these "wholes?" Are we able to fulfill this "as"? We truly do not have even half of these "wholes." When we are happy, we may love God a little, and when our neighbor pleases us, we may love him a little. We cannot even love our parents, let alone our neighbors. Hence, God gave the law of the Old Testament in order to show man's inability, incompetence, and incapability.

THE LAW OF THE NEW TESTAMENT PROVES THAT WITH MAN IT IS IMPOSSIBLE, BUT WITH GOD ALL THINGS ARE POSSIBLE

This is the situation with the commandments of the Old Testament, but how about that of the New Testament? The commandments and laws of the New Testament are different from those of the Old Testament. The commandments and laws of the New Testament are to prove that God is able, to prove that with men it is impossible, but with God all things are possible. The Lord said to the disciples in Matthew 19:24, "It is easier for a camel to pass through the eye of a needle than for a rich man to enter into the kingdom of God." It is hard for a big camel to pass through the eye of a needle. After the disciples heard this word, they asked, "Who then can be saved?" This was the conclusion of the disciples, but the Lord Jesus said, "With men this is impossible, but with God all things are possible" (v. 26).

With men this is impossible refers to the law; *with God all things are possible* refers to grace. It is impossible for man to take care of the vineyard, to plant the vine trees, and to bear fruit for man's enjoyment, but it is possible for God to prepare a feast with a rich supply of wine for man to enjoy. We have to bear in mind that the commandments of the Old Testament are to show us that with men it is impossible, while the commandments of the New Testament are to show us that with God everything is possible and that everything hinges on God Himself.

The Old Testament is a matter of the law, and there is no way for man to fulfill the law by himself. The New Testament is not just a matter of the law; rather, it opens the way for man to receive the life of God, which is Christ Himself entering into man and supplying man to meet the requirement of God in man. In the New Testament, however much God demands of man, this much He will supply to man; however, in the Old Testament, whatever God demanded of man only indicated how incapable man was. In the New Testament age whenever we touch God and have fellowship with God, all our impossibilities become possibilities and all our inabilities become abilities.

There is a portion in the Bible that records the miracle of the Lord Jesus feeding five thousand (14:14-21). On that day, apart from the women and children, there were about five thousand men. The disciples told the Lord Jesus, "The hour is already late. Send the crowds away that they may go into the villages and buy food for themselves" (v. 15). But the Lord Jesus said, "You give them something to eat" (v. 16). This was the Lord's strict command, but the disciples replied that they did not know where to get them food. If the story ended here, then the Lord's command would be the law—the Old Testament. However, the Lord's word here is not the Old Testament but the New Testament, not the law but grace. To be more specific, the Lord's word here was not a command but an indication, showing man the way to receive more of God's abundant grace. When we ourselves do not have anything to eat, how can we feed others? The Lord then asked them, "How many loaves do you have?" (Mark 6:38). They said, "Five, and two fish." Then the Lord took the five loaves and the two fish, blessed them, and gave them to the disciples, the disciples gave them to the crowds, and they all ate and were satisfied. This proves that behind the demand of the Lord Jesus, there is a great supply.

After a person is saved, he has to confess his sins, deal with his sins and conscience, and consecrate himself to the Lord. None of these things can be done by ourselves. However, should we stop here? If we stop here, all these matters will be laws to us. We should not stop here; rather, we should bring all our inability and incapability to the Lord and tell Him, "O Lord, You want me to deal with my sins and conscience, but I cannot do it." By coming to the Lord in this way, we will see how much the power of God and the abundant grace of Christ can do in us.

THE COMMANDMENTS OF THE NEW TESTAMENT OPENING THE WAY TO THE GRACE OF GOD

The Old Testament causes man to see his inability, while the New Testament is the way God opens His grace to man. Whenever man realizes that he is poor, he will be open to receive the supply of God's abundant grace. In short, every commandment and demand of God is to prove man's inability and incapability. Whenever we bring all these commandments and demands to God, He immediately opens the way to transmit His supply to us continually.

There was once a wife who felt that she should confess to her husband. This was very hard for her to do because she was used to being a domineering wife. Her will was very

strong and she was very proud. Usually it is the wife who fears
the husband, but in this case it was her husband who feared
her. One day, however, she felt that she was wrong and that
she should confess to her husband. Yet when she considered
doing it, she encountered a few problems. First, she did not
have much strength; second, she was afraid of losing her face;
and third, because she had oppressed her husband in the
past, she was afraid that her husband would turn around and
oppress her. At that point she felt that she could no longer be
a Christian. She knew that being a Christian meant that she
had to be enlightened by the Lord. She also knew that after
she was enlightened by the Lord, she would have to deal with
all the unpeaceful feelings within her conscience; if she did
not, she would feel even more unpeaceful. So she decided, "I
will just be a casual Christian; I will just be what I am." This
kind of Christian is a typical Christian. Their heart is very
sincere, their words are true, and they feel sorrowful within.

How can we help people like this? We have to help them to
know that all the commandments of the New Testament open
the way to the grace of God. Whenever we receive a command
from God, we should bring it back to Him and tell Him, "O
God, I cannot do it; I give You this command just as the disciples gave You the five loaves and two fish. I am always
incapable. I give Your command and myself to You. Lord, do
whatever you think is good. I cannot do anything at all."
Those who practice coming to the Lord in such a way will be
blessed and will receive the bountiful supply from the Lord.
This can be compared to the disciples bringing the five loaves
and two fish to the Lord. As soon as they did this, the riches
were manifested.

Do not think that the miracle of five loaves and two fish is
the only miracle. Every time that God leads us to obey His
command, it is also a miracle. If the Lord does not perform a
miracle in us, we cannot do anything and we do not have anything. We may be at our end, yet the Lord causes the dead to
be resurrected. Every time that we keep the Lord's command,
He definitely is performing a great miracle in us.

We should always believe God, because He would never
wrong us. If we feel that we have wronged our husband, we

should confess our sins to him. If we cannot do it, we have to give ourselves to the Lord. The Lord will absolutely take care of the result. We do not need to be anxious or to doubt anything. The Lord's grace is wonderful! We are not able to do many things, but after we pray, consecrate ourselves to the Lord, and put ourselves into the Lord's gracious hands, there will be an indescribable force welling up within us urging us to confess. We may not even utter anything, but our tears will flow down. As this is happening, we will not feel ashamed at all. We will only feel that we are filled with God and that we are full of strength. Perhaps for this reason the person that we are confessing to may be saved.

AS LONG AS WE ARE WILLING, GOD IS ABLE

All the commandments of the New Testament are the same as the laws of the Old Testament—they are God's demand on man, requiring man to do something. God's demands in the New Testament, however, are not meant to be fulfilled by man alone but are meant to be fulfilled by God Himself. How can we ask a patient with tuberculosis to walk to Kaohsiung? If he wants to go to Kaohsiung, we have to let him fly or at least go by train. We should not allow him to exert any energy. Today many children of God do not understand that God's New Testament commandments and grace are altogether not a matter of our ability, but a matter of our willingness. If we are willing, we will bring all our inability and incapability to God. As long as we are willing, God is able. When we place ourselves into the hands of God, He will have a way to perform "signs and wonders" in us.

If we find it burdensome to confess our sins, to deal with our sins and conscience, and to consecrate ourselves to the Lord, we should not lose heart. In the New Testament, as long as we are willing to obey God's demand and put ourselves in the hands of God, God will enable us in the midst of our inability. Then we will be able to see God's presence, God's grace, and God's eternal glory.

Chapter Nine

BEING ABLE TO DO ALL THINGS IN CHRIST

John 15:5 says, "I am the vine; you are the branches. He who abides in Me and I in him, he bears much fruit; for apart from Me you can do nothing." Philippians 4:11-13 says, "Not that I speak according to lack, for I have learned, in whatever circumstances I am, to be content. I know also how to be abased, and I know how to abound; in everything and in all things I have learned the secret both to be filled and to hunger, both to abound and to lack. I am able to do all things in Him who empowers me." Verse 13 has the phrase, "I am able to do all things in Him who empowers me." We all know that *Him who empowers me* refers to Christ. We are able to do all things in Him who empowers us.

ALL THE SAVED ONES
HAVING A HEART TO PLEASE GOD

Every saved one has a heart to please God. This heart is very strong in some people but very weak in others. Nevertheless, whether this heart is strong or weak, all the saved ones do have such a heart, unless one never thinks about God or seeks God. Once a person seeks God, spontaneously he has a heart to please God. This is because in this universe God desires that man have a heart to love Him and seek after Him.

All those who know God know that God has much grace for man and much work to do in man. Yet if man does not want this, God will have no way to do anything. Thus, for men to give their heart to God is to provide Him a way to work in them. If a person is not willing to give his heart to God, God will have no way to grace him or to work in him. This may be illustrated by parents who want to do something for their children, yet their children turn their back on them and turn away from them. As a result, the parents are not able to do anything. A heart that loves God is very precious to God and is what God treasures. God desires that man would love Him and seek after Him. This does not mean that God wants to gain something good from man, but rather that God has many good things for man, much grace to grant man, and much work to do in man. If man does not love God or draw near to Him, God will have no way to do what He desires, so God always desires that man love Him and draw near to Him.

In the same way that parents do, God continually longs that His children be like Him. Whenever there is a heart that turns back to God, He treasures it very much. Many times, however, because we do not desire Him that much, He has to use some winding ways to turn us back to Him. Every time we feel the love of God and the sweetness of God's love within us, our love toward God spontaneously wells up, and we pray, "O God, I love You; my heart is here for You." We feel that God is so lovely and so precious. So we pray to God, "O God, You are the most precious One; nothing is more precious than You. Although there are many things that are lovely, when they are compared with You, You are the most glorious One. O God, I do not care whether or not I am able to love You; I simply love You, and I will love You forever."

GOD REQUIRING MAN TO LOVE HIM WITH MAN'S HEART, BUT NOT WITH MAN'S OWN STRENGTH

The fact that we can pray such a prayer proves that God has worked in us. Sometimes God uses the outward environment to compel us to love Him; this is God's work. Sometimes He draws us with His love; this is also God's work. God does these things because He wants us to love Him. God cannot do much in a person who has never allowed God to work in him and does not feel that God is loveable. Whenever God works in a person, He first lets the person see that He is lovely. As a result, this person's heart rises up. Then this person will love God. This is something very precious.

However, whenever someone is willing to rise up to love God, a great problem appears. Everyone, without exception, has this same problem. As soon as a person rises up to love God, a problem will appear right away—this person will try his best to please God. The desire to love God and please God is very proper and precious and is absolutely acceptable to God. Yet this person will love God with his own strength and in his own way. This is what displeases God. God does not want anything that is from our own strength and rejects everything that is of our own strength.

For example, I may ask a brother to do a certain thing with me, but I do not want him to use his own effort because this will be a great problem. It sounds very strange to say that we ask people to help us but that we do not want them to use their own strength. If someone asks you to help him to do something but does not want you to use your strength, this will be very hard for you to do. It would be very troublesome to you if this person wants your heart, but he does not want your wisdom or your way. Normally, if a person asks me to help him, I would help him in my own way and with my own wisdom and strength. But if he does not want my strength, wisdom, or way, why would he want my help? I had better not go to help him. To use our own strength is a human principle. However, this is not God's way. He does not want man to bring his own strength, ways, or wisdom. God wants only man's heart.

CEASING FROM OUR STRENGTH AND METHODS AND LEAVING EVERYTHING TO HIM

About fifteen years ago I met a Western missionary who shared with me his testimony. He said that although he was saved when he was young, he did not know the Lord adequately. Even though he had come to China to do missionary work, he still did not know the Lord much. He used an illustration of driving a car to explain this. He said that since he was not a good driver, he asked the Lord to help him. The Lord was like his Advisor. Every time he was perplexed, he asked the Lord for advice. When he did not have any strength, he asked the Lord to help him. This was his past situation. Still, he did not think that the Lord had helped him very much. It seemed that the more he asked the Lord for direction, the more the Lord refused to give him direction. Later he became clear that although his love for the Lord was right, he should not use his own effort or methods; he had to stop all his own effort and methods. He knew that it was right to have a heart for the Lord and that without such a heart the Lord would have no way to grant him grace or to work in him. He realized, however, that he would have to put his own methods and strength aside. He said that he would now give "the whole car" to the Lord, including the seats and the steering wheel. When the Lord drove well, he would praise the Lord; when the Lord drove fast, he would thank the Lord. He handed his whole life over into the Lord's hands. He would just sit next to the Lord and enjoy. All the problems would be taken care of by the Lord, and all the strength would come from the Lord, while he would just look at the scenery and enjoy it.

Although this is a simple illustration, it shows us the problem that many people have. Either we do not love God, or once we love God, we use our own effort and methods to please Him. As a result we deviate from God. We want to love God and please God with our own strength, according to our own view, and in our own way; however, God does not want any of this. As a result, eventually we will deviate from God. Hence, many times when we are weak, we ask God to strengthen us. Many times when we fail, we ask God to cause us to overcome and to help us to stand firm. This kind of prayer is seldom answered. God hardly ever answers prayers for strengthening or overcoming. Hence, many people may doubt God and ask, "Why didn't God listen to my prayer?" The problem is that if you are the one who is driving the car, and you ask the Lord to be your Advisor or Helper, the Lord would never give you any advice or help. There is a saying which is very true: If we do not allow the Lord to work completely, the Lord will not work. If we use our own way to please God, we will be distracted from God and may even be discouraged. Many distractions and problems come from this, but this is also the time for us to receive grace. For this reason, God always particularly arranges the environment in order to weaken us and make us feel that we cannot bear or handle the environment.

GOD RAISING UP THE ENVIRONMENT TO BREAK US

If we are those who already love God, then we may ask Him to help us to do better in order to please Him. In response, God not only will not help us, but He will worsen our environment to suppress us and cause us to be unable to do anything. At a time like this, many people may wonder why it is that before they loved God, they did not have any problems; however, now that they love God, their environment has become more difficult. This is exactly what God is doing. It is because we have a heart to love God that He raises up the environment in order to break our effort and all of our methods. God does not want any of our effort or ways; He wants only our heart.

This is the hardest part of God's work in man. Many times, when our heart comes, our strength also comes. The two seem to be inseparable. Yet God wants only man's heart, not man's effort or ways. This problem is similar to a doctor operating on a patient who has a tumor. The tumor, which is connected to the patient's body, has to be removed, but his body has to be preserved. When we do not love God, our strength does not come. When we do not love God, the adverse environment also will not rise up. However, once we love God, our strength comes. In order for God to perfect our heart and break our strength, He allows situations to come to us. Hence, many people are confused, yet our God is never confused. Whenever God works in us, He always gives us an inner sense through which He charges us to please Him. However, although God gives us such a sense and commands us to please Him. He does not want us to please Him by ourselves. He wants the Lord Jesus to be our strength to please Him. Therefore, God worsens our environment in order to break us so that we will be unable to rely on ourselves.

A Christian sister, who was accustomed to not submitting to her husband, read from the Bible one day that wives should respect their husbands and be subject to them. In response, she had a heart to respect her husband and be subject to him, so she made a resolution before God, saying, "O God, from now on give me the strength that I may respect my husband and submit myself to him." Her prayer, on the one hand, shows her desire to please God, but on the other hand, it shows that she intended to use her own effort to submit herself to her husband. She loved God and wanted to please God, but she intended to use her own effort to obey her husband and thus to please God, so she prayed and asked God for help. What did God do? Eight out of ten times, God made her husband's temper even bigger and worse than before. Every day she prayed, "O God, give me the strength to obey my husband." God not only did not give her the strength, but He allowed her husband's temper to get worse. This caused her to be discouraged, and so she prayed again before God, "O God, in the past when I did not obey Your word, my husband was like a lamb. Now that I want to please You, he has become worse. I wonder why this is so." Finally, she was not able to pray any more. What was happening? We have to bear in mind that for a wife to submit to her husband depends on God. In addition, it is also God's doing when the husbands lose their temper. God does such things simply because He wants our strength to go bankrupt.

I met a sister who, after her salvation, took good care of her husband at home. Although outwardly she did not show pride in her face, she did expose a flavor of pride in her speaking. One day she encountered a problem. She wanted to love God, so she prayed, "O God, from now on, I want to please You in dealing with my husband and my children." After she prayed such a prayer, her family situation became chaotic, her husband's temper was worse, and her children were naughtier. She prayed that she would be a submissive wife to her husband and a good mother to her children in order to please God, but her family situation became more and more difficult. She was almost unable to bear it, and she felt that she did not look proper at home at all. So she came to me and said, "Brother, what is happening? In the past when I was a typical sister, my family situation was not that bad; at least I looked like a good wife before my husband and a good mother before my children. But since the day I decided to love God and please God in dealing with my husband and children, they became harder to deal with. They cannot take it, and neither can I." This is not merely our sister's problem but the problem of many of us.

If we love God, it is His doing, and if we have turmoil in our family, it is also His doing. All these things come together for the purpose of bringing our strength to an end. Whether we are humble or kind, our humbleness and kindness are both from our own strength. If we are not broken, even if we are good, whatever we do will be nothing but our own doing, rather than God's doing it in us and through us, or our doing it through God. The things that we do may be right, but if our being is wrong, our strength will also be wrong. Therefore, God raises up the environment to break us and eliminate our strength. If we try to please God not according to His way, He will raise up the environment to eliminate our strength and ruin our way, so that all we have left is a heart to please Him, not our own effort or way. When we are brought to this point, all we will be able to do is prostrate ourselves before God and say, "O God, I do not have any strength to please You. O God, it is impossible to please You with my own strength and according to my own way. O God, the most I have is just a heart to love You and desire You."

BEING DELIVERED FROM THE SELF
AND LIVING IN CHRIST

At this moment, we will live before God, and at this time, God will show us the glorious fact that apart from the Lord we can do nothing. Apart from the Lord whatever we do cannot please God. Only when the Lord becomes our strength are we able to please God. In John 15:5 the Lord said, "For apart from Me you can do nothing." On the one hand, the Bible shows us that we are able to do all things in Him who empowers us (Phil. 4:13), and on the other hand, it says that apart from Christ we can do nothing. This means that not only do we need to be delivered from ourselves, but we also need to be in Christ. In other words, God is breaking us so that we would not rely on ourselves and would be delivered from the self;

He is also showing us that Christ is both our strength and our power.

It is through this kind of process that our strength goes bankrupt, and it is also through such an experience that God shows us that Christ is our strength and that He is living and powerful within us. For this reason we can testify that it is "no longer I...but...Christ" (Gal. 2:20). At this time, we will praise and thank the Lord from within, and we will tell the Lord, "Lord, You are my life, and You are my power." We will put ourselves aside and say, "Lord, we have Your life and Your power in us. We would not use our own strength or method any more." This is the holy living of a Christian, and this is the overcoming living of a Christian. We do not need to resolve to be submissive, because there is a power which enables us to be submissive. There is no need to make a resolution, because the power, which is just the Lord Himself, comes from within. At this point we will realize that everything we do is not merely good but is the Lord Himself.

APART FROM CHRIST WE CAN DO NOTHING

The power of God is Christ, but in our experience several steps are needed for Christ to express His power from within us. The first step is that He draws our heart to love Him. The second step is that we try to love Him by ourselves, but we fail and are discouraged. Then at this very moment God shows us that it is not our own strength but Christ's; it is not we but Christ; it is not our way but Christ's; it is not our wisdom but Christ's. God shows us that we have to put our own effort and methods aside. Then even though we do not do it intentionally, we put ourselves aside, because we have had so many failures which have caused us to lose our self-confidence. While other people are able to overcome, we cannot; we fail incessantly. We realize that people like us are not able to please God. At this point we are broken; we are thoroughly broken. We see that it is no longer we but Christ. Only when we are in Christ are we able to do all things. In this way the Lord Jesus spontaneously becomes the power in us. All the holiness and overcoming that we will have will have come through this breaking process.

When a person becomes zealous for the Lord and wants to do many things for the Lord, I always have two different feelings. On the one hand, I feel that it is always good for someone to have the willingness to serve the Lord; on the other hand, I have the feeling that his zeal is not of much use and that he is destined to fail. Not only so, failing and falling are good for a Christian.

There was a saint whose situation and prayer were good before he got married. But after he was married, he was not able to read the Bible or fellowship with God properly because he had a problem before God. He did not understand why this was the case. Before he was married, he did not have any problem with the Lord; once he married, not only was he unable to pray, but he was also discouraged within. If he did not go to the meetings, his inner being would disagree, but if he went to the meetings, his inner being would be discouraged. He knew that he had to love the Lord, but he was not able to do so. He was depressed to the uttermost. When I saw this situation, I was really joyful. He asked me what he should do, and I told him that he did not need to do anything or worry about anything. This was nothing but the Lord's breaking him.

We often think that we are able to please the Lord with our own strength. However, man's effort plus man's methods merely represent the self. When we try to please God in this way, it is our own power, not the life of Christ. It is our own way, not Christ's enlightening. It is we who are expressed, not Christ. It is we who are trying to please God, not Christ pleasing God. In this way, Christ Himself is not expressed, and there is no way for Christ to be expressed as our life and power. We have to know that the Christian life is not to do good but to express Christ. God's purpose is to work Christ into us that He would be expressed from within us.

Every time we make a resolution to please God, we have to realize that what follows will always be discipline, failures, and bankruptcy. This bankruptcy does not refer to something physical but to something ethical. We will be unable to stand hardships. The environment will be raised up by God to suppress us, to break us, to cause us to be disappointed in ourself, and to esteem ourselves as nothing. At this moment, we will see that we cannot please God by our own strength. What pleases God is what Christ does through us; what pleases God is when Christ gains ground in us. However, for Christ to gain ground in us and be expressed through us, we have to allow our strength, our methods, and our wisdom to be broken by God.

NO LONGER I BUT CHRIST

The majority of people think that man's problem is sin and that sin is the enemy of God. In fact, man's problem is not sin but his own strength and his own way. It is because man has too much strength, too many ways, and too much wisdom that Christ does not have any ground in him. For Christ to gain ground in man, God has to do one thing. What is that one thing? He has to break the human strength, methods, wisdom, and determination. All of man's strength, methods, wisdom, and determination have to be broken by God.

Our experience tells us that the more we struggle, the more breaking there will be. The more we pray to ask God to fulfill our desire to please Him, the more God will break us. God will particularly create situations that we are not able to stand; eventually, all our strength and methods will go bankrupt because we will not be able to bear the environment. Both our strength and methods will go bankrupt. Then we will say, "O God, I cannot do it. I do not have anything other than a heart that loves You." At this time God will show us that the Lord Jesus is living in us to be our life and our strength. Then we will prostrate ourselves and say, "O God, it is no longer I but Christ; it is no longer my methods but Your leading; it is no longer my determination but Your shining." As a result we will be able to please God, and Christ will be able to fill us within and be expressed without. Whoever has reached such an extent has had to pass through many sufferings and breakings. Blessed are those who can pass through all these sufferings and breakings. In this way we will know how Christ can be the power in us. Apart from Christ we can do nothing, but we are able to do all things in Him.

CHAPTER TEN

SOME NECESSARY DEALINGS
IN THE SERVICE OF GOD

DISCERNING DESIRE, INTENTION, AND ABILITY

One who serves God must learn to discern three things: desire, intention, and ability. We all know that a desire is something which man longs for. An intention, to many people, refers to what man hopes for. And of course, we all know that ability refers to the strength we need to accomplish a certain matter. A person who serves the Lord must be dealt with in these three matters, or there will be a lack in his service.

The desire to serve God is indispensable for every serving one. What God treasures the most is man's desire to serve Him and man's desire for Him. God created the universe and all things, but His heart is not on the sun or the stars. Neither is His heart on the angels or on all the other things, because none of these things are for God. The Bible tells us that man is the center of the universe (cf. Zech. 12:1), and that without man the purpose of God cannot be accomplished. Hence, even though God has created all things, His real concern and focus is man alone. The hardest thing for God to gain in man is his heart. This may be likened to a father who loves his son more than anything else but is not able to gain his son's heart. For us to cooperate with someone, our heart must be open to that person. God has a great deal of work that He desires to do in the universe, but He must gain the cooperation of man to accomplish His work. Hence, to do this, He has to touch man's heart.

GOD DESIRING MAN'S HEART TO LOVE HIM

How does God touch man's heart? What method does He

use to move our heart? He uses His love to move our heart. What is love? Love is God's heart. The heart is really a special thing. When we talk about the heart, we usually refer to love. The heart does not respond to thinking; it must be touched by love. God created us with a heart that we may feel such love. For example, when we are thirsty and someone gives us a glass of water, we drink it. But when we are not thirsty, no matter how much water people give us, we would not drink it. God's heart is like the glass of water, and our heart is the thirst. Everyone responds to love because in man there is a heart of love. We have a body without and a spirit within, and in between our spirit and our body is the soul, which includes the mind, the emotion, and the will.

God's heart desires that man would love Him, but man's heart always loves something other than God, something that he should not love. Regardless of our age—old or young—some love their families, some love their pets, some love movies, some love to play mah-jongg, some love their reputation, some love position, some love knowledge, and some love money. It seems that without love, man has no meaning. The wonderful thing is that once man has love, he is willing to do anything. Without love, however, it is difficult for him even to lift a finger. No matter how dirty a child is, his mother is willing to take care of him because she loves him. A maid, however, may not be able to render the same care. If we read the Bible in a serious way, we should know that God's first demand on man is his heart, and second, his love. From the very beginning until the end, God just wants man to be for Him, and God desires that man would love Him with his heart.

The most legitimate love is the love for God Himself. If our heart loves anything else, sooner or later we will suffer loss. Many people who love money are eventually bitten by money. Many people who love others are cheated by them. The Bible tells us that only those who love God really taste the sweetness. Psalm 43:4 says, "And I will go to the altar of God, / To God my exceeding joy." To those whose heart is turned to God, God is their joy. Some people love God so much that just hearing the name of God causes them to feel like they have received an electric shock. This is the kind of heart toward Him that God desires.

However, once we turn our heart to God and we are prepared to live for God, a problem will come. If a person has love, then he will also have an opinion. We may use as an illustration a time when I went to a certain place, and the saints there loved me very much. When they ate, they liked to put sesame oil in every single dish of food or bowl of soup. Thus, the more sesame oil they put into your dish, the more they welcomed you. However, I did not like sesame oil; whenever I smelled sesame oil, I could not stand it. Yet at that time I had no choice but to eat it because we who work for the Lord have to keep a principle that wherever we go, we eat whatever people serve us. Not only did they put sesame oil in my food, but regardless of whether I slept or went out, there was always a brother with me. As a result, I could not rest well or come near to God. They really loved much, but this kind of love was unbearable.

DENYING THE SELF

This example shows us that once a person loves God, his opinions and proposals will follow and that once his opinions and proposals come, God will suffer. For example, if someone loves you according to his own opinion and never pays attention to your feeling, you will only suffer from this kind of love. Peter was just like this in Matthew 16. His love for the Lord was right, but his good intention in rebuking the Lord was not right. His good heart was right, but his good intention was not right. God wants man's heart but not man's opinion. Do you love your husband? The secret of love is that you do not do things according to your own intention and will but according to his intention and his will. If those saints who loved me really knew what love is, they would have asked me whether or not I eat sesame oil instead of insisting on putting sesame oil in my food. In Matthew 16 Peter did have a good intention, yet the Lord said, "Get behind Me, Satan!" (v. 23). Today many people love the Lord and are zealous for the Lord, but their good intentions have never been broken by the Lord. They cast out demons in the Lord's name, but the

Lord does not approve of them because they do it according to their own intention and preference, and not according to the Lord's intention and preference. They do not take care of God's preference but man's preference.

Therefore, the Lord said, "If anyone wants to come after Me, let him deny himself and take up his cross and follow Me" (v. 24). To forsake the self is to deny the self. The function of the cross is to put the self to death. Many times when we do not love the Lord very much, we do not have that many problems, but the more we love the Lord, the more sufferings we have. When they gave me sesame oil, I could refrain from saying anything; however, one day their "giving of sesame oil" will be broken by God. I suffered, not because of their love, but because of their opinion. We must see that the cross comes to deal with our opinion. The life and work of every fallen man is always directed by his thinking, and if his thinking is strong, it becomes his opinion. Due to the fall, man's opinion has become the strongest factor in directing his living and move.

Man's heart loves the Lord, but man's way of thinking has never been broken by the Lord. For this reason, God always breaks us. Some are willing to receive such a breaking, while others withdraw when they suffer a blow. For example, some sisters really love the Lord, and they are willing to serve in the meeting hall. But once their heart is stirred up, their opinion also comes. One example of this is cleaning the chairs in the meeting hall. Even in this service two different people will have two different opinions. One says that she wants to clean the chairs with a dry cloth, while another insists that she use a damp cloth. Finally, the one who suggests using a dry cloth would say, "All right. If you insist that your opinion is right, then I will leave. You clean the chairs by yourself." Does this sister love the church? Of course she loves the church. But if she loves the church, why did she leave? She left because the other sister did not clean the chairs according to her opinion. Opinions can be a problem even in the preaching of the gospel. All the saints are zealous and are willing to rise up to join the gospel team for the preaching of the gospel. One brother, however, says that the gospel drums should be beaten in his way, and if others do not accept his opinion, he will not come again. We all have to learn the lesson that in all our service we should bring our heart but not our opinion.

The service of the church does not depend on the accomplishment of tasks but on the perfecting of the person who serves. Time is God's servant. Thus, we all need to receive God's dealing while we are in time so that we will be the kind of people that God desires. In the preaching of the gospel and in the work, everything hinges on how much dealing we have received. We may use the sisters who clean the chairs as an example. The sister who takes the lead may not be as good as you, because you are smart and capable. Your opinion may be very good, so if the sisters do not listen to you, you will not come again. If this is the case, you not only do not know how to do things, but you do not even know how to conduct yourself as a proper human being. The lesson of the cross is that even though my opinion may be right, I do not pay attention to my own opinion; all I know is to love the Lord. When I come to clean the chairs, I would like to clean away all my opinions and disposition. If at home you love your husband, and your husband loves you to the extent that he even lets you put the chairs upside down, then in this situation it is hard for you to be broken. The greatest function of the cross is to break your proposals, your opinions, and your being.

In the matter of service we often do things according to our own opinions. In addition, the more we love the Lord, the more opinions we have. The flesh is hidden in our love for the Lord. How do we know this? It is because our flesh is hidden in our opinions, and our opinions are, in fact, sugarcoated poison. When people do not accept our opinions, our flesh will be expressed right away. If we do something well, but people insist on saying that we did not do it well, our flesh will immediately be expressed in our temper. Everyone is the same. Before we ask a person for help, he does not have any opinions; however, once we ask him for help, all his opinions will come with him. When love comes, opinions follow. However, once our opinions come, God will come to break them. Some people, due to their fear of God's breaking, withdraw their love. There was once a brother who loved the Lord and was willing to offer his money and effort to the church, yet the brothers with whom he met were not very nice to him. This caused him to be discouraged. In terms of serving, it may have been the brothers who did not see things accurately, and perhaps he was right; however, in terms of his person, it was the Lord who wanted to deal with him through the brothers.

When we read the four Gospels, we see that Peter loved to give his opinions and always made mistakes. In Matthew 17, one day the Lord and His disciples went to Capernaum. While the Lord was in the house, those who took the temple tax came and asked Peter, "Does not your Teacher pay the temple tax?" Peter answered them without any hesitation and said, "Yes." Here we see that he gave his opinion and left his position. He should have returned to the house and asked the Lord whether or not He would pay the tax. Peter did not ask the Lord but said, "Yes." So when he entered into the house, the Lord asked him, "From whom do the kings of the earth receive custom or poll tax, from their sons or from strangers?" Peter replied, "From strangers." Then the Lord said, "So then the sons are free" (vv. 24-26). However, for the sake of not stumbling others, the Lord paid the tax. When Peter said, "Yes," the Lord said, "No." And when Peter said, "No," the Lord said, "Yes." The Lord did this intentionally to deal with Peter. In addition, how did they pay the tax? The way they paid the tax was by the Lord's asking Peter to go fishing. This really troubled Peter. The Lord told him to take the first fish that he caught, to take a stater out from its mouth, and then to take that to pay the tax (v. 27). This is very meaningful. If I were Peter, I would have been perplexed. Why did the Lord deal with Peter in such a way? The Lord mainly did this to deal with Peter's opinions because Peter always spoke first. However, in Acts we see that Peter had been dealt with. By this time he had been thoroughly dealt with and did not have any opinions. When the rulers of the people came, took Peter and John away, and forbade them to preach based upon the name of Jesus, Peter said to them that although they asked him not to speak, if God wanted him to speak, he would have to speak (Acts 4:18-20). His heart and his thinking had been dealt with by God.

In the Old Testament, King David felt that he should

prepare a sanctuary for God since he himself dwelt in a house of cedar. Hence, he set the Ark of God upon an ox cart, brought it out of the house of Abinadab from Baale-judah, and carried it to the city of David. On the way, when they came to Nachon's threshing floor, the oxen stumbled and the Ark of God began to fall over, so Uzzah reached out and took hold of the Ark. When he did so, he was struck by God. After Uzzah died, David wondered if he had done something wrong. Later, he understood that this happened because God does not like man's strength. As a result, the next time David had the priests bear the Ark of Jehovah. When they had gone six paces, David sacrificed an ox and a fatling, girded himself with an ephod, and danced with all his might before Jehovah (2 Sam. 6:1-15). This story shows us how God rejects man's thought and man's ability.

SIMPLY LOVING THE LORD AFTER BEING DEALT WITH

On the night that the Lord told the disciples that they would all be stumbled because of Him, Peter said to the Lord, "If all will be stumbled because of You, I will never be stumbled" (Matt. 26:33). Right after he said such a word, God specially raised up an environment to strike his pride. When the Lord was being taken away after being arrested, Peter followed Him at a distance, and while the Lord was being tortured cruelly by the high priest, Peter warmed himself in the courtyard. While he was there, a servant girl came up to him and said, "You also were with Jesus the Galilean" (v. 69). Peter denied this immediately. On that night the Lord's word that Peter would deny Him three times was fulfilled. Through this experience Peter was dealt with and was distressed to the uttermost. As a result, later he went fishing.

After the Lord was resurrected, He manifested Himself to Peter at the Sea of Tiberias and said to him, "Do you love Me?" This time Peter did not answer the Lord directly, saying, "I love You," but instead he said, "Yes, Lord, You know that I love You" (John 21:16). Although Peter loved the Lord, he realized that his speaking did not mean anything. So when the Lord asked him the third time, "Simon, son of John, do you love Me?" Peter was grieved, and he said to the Lord, "Lord,

You know all things; You know that I love You" (v. 17). At this point Peter really had lost all his confidence. He did love the Lord very much, but he had no more confidence in himself. Before he had said in a bold way that he would not be stumbled, yet he was stumbled three times in a single day. On that day at the Sea of Tiberias, the fact that the Lord asked him three times, "Do you love Me," really has a special meaning. On the day that he denied the Lord, Peter was warming himself in the courtyard of the high priest, but on this day the Lord prepared the fire for him at the Sea of Tiberias. Formerly, Peter went fishing for his living, but on this day the Lord gave him fish to eat. Before Peter needed to start the fire; now the Lord prepared the fire for him. Before Peter needed to fish for his living; now the Lord roasted a fish for him. At the Sea of Tiberius the Lord came in person to touch Peter's heart, and once the Lord's love came, all Peter's natural power was gone.

However, when Peter saw the disciple whom the Lord loved, reclining on Jesus' breast, his opinion came out again, and he asked, "Lord, and what about this man?" (v. 21). In response, the Lord dealt with him again, saying, "If I want him to remain until I come, what is that to you? You follow Me" (v. 22). Before saying this, the Lord also had said to Peter, "When you were younger, you girded yourself and walked where you wished; but when you grow old, you will stretch out your hands, and another will gird you and carry you where you do not wish to go" (v. 18). The Lord wanted Peter not to pay attention to how other people would be, but to just follow Him. This is the last dealing that Peter had. Peter's flesh and way of thinking were all dealt with. He did not have any more opinions or any more self. Therefore, on the day of Pentecost Peter was not the same; he was absolutely another person. Even when people did not want him to speak, he continued to speak for the Lord's testimony. He was entirely without the self. Eventually, God's will broke Peter's will, and the death of the cross subdued Peter's opinions and strength. It is said that eventually Peter was even willing to be crucified for the Lord upside down.